DATE DUE

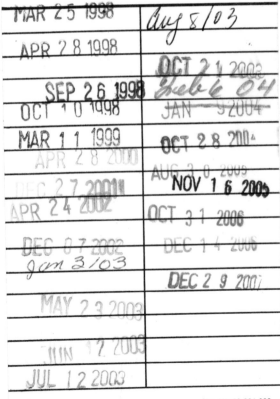

MAR 25 1998	Aug 8/03
APR 2 8 1998	
	OCT 2 1 2003
SEP 2 6 1998	Feb 6 04
OCT 1 0 1998	JAN 9 2004
MAR 1 1 1999	OCT 2 8 2004
APR 2 8 2000	AUG 3 0 2005
DEC 2 7 2001	NOV 1 6 2005
APR 2 4 2002	OCT 3 1 2006
DEC 0 7 2002	DEC 1 4 2006
Jan 3/03	
	DEC 2 9 2007
MAY 2 3 2003	
JUN 1 2 2003	
JUL 1 2 2003	

Paul St. Pierre

CHILCOTIN AND BEYOND

DOUGLAS & McINTYRE
VANCOUVER/TORONTO

Douglas & McIntyre
1615 Venables Street
Vancouver, British Columbia V5L 2H1

Canadian Cataloguing in Publication Data
St. Pierre, Paul, 1923–
   Chilcotin and beyond

   ISBN 0-88894-673-2

   I. Title.
PS8537.A54C55   1989   C813'.54   C89-091523-7
PR9199.3.S16C55   1989

Most of the articles in this book, some in slightly different form, originally appeared in the *Vancouver Sun* and *The New York Times*.

Design by Gabriele Proctor
Typeset by The Typeworks

Printed and bound in Canada

This book is dedicated to Yésica,
my Mexican-born daughter.

Contents

|||

Prologue

|||

IN our Mexican home we have for a friend and neighbour an old man named Jesus who works about fourteen hours of every day, yet finds extra time to guide the sun across our garden by day and set the big tropic stars in their places over our heads at night.

Not long ago he said to my wife, "I have known you two for many years, but you know I'm still not sure what Paul does."

"Paul writes books," said my wife.

Jesus said, "Oh, I know that . . . but . . . he can DO things too, can't he?"

It repeated all too exactly the question of an acquaintance in Chilcotin who asked me what I did on the *Sun*. I told him I wrote a column. "I know you write columns," he said. "What I was asking was, what is your regular work on the paper?"

I should have told him, as my wife should have told Jesus, that writing, which seems simple, really consists of peering at a blank screen on a word processor until drops of blood come out on your forehead.

That would have been a good response. But would it have been true? No.

For most of my working life I spent only little bits of time in actually committing labour. As a newspaper columnist, most of my days were used up in taking holidays at the expense of the *Vancouver Sun*. Many of the *Sun* columns appeared in the predecessor to this book, *Chilcotin Holiday*, and more are here.

Since *Chilcotin Holiday* appeared in a revised edition in 1984, I have retired from the newspaper business. That hasn't made much difference. I don't talk as much about the really big projects I'm going to start tomorrow, but that's about all. I continue to write and to profit from it. I keep trying to quell, if not quench, the suspicion that writing is not a proper way for a grown man to earn a living. I continue my sojourns in the cattle country of Chilcotin where I still find people who have achieved the perfect blend of earthy common sense and madly improbable dreams.

However, I had a land hunger which was unsatisfied in Chilcotin. What I wanted was a small corner of some small place where the rest of the world would not see, know or care about me.

There are scarcely any small bits of private land to be bought in the remoter parts of the plateau. And the Crown lands sold to individuals many years ago, during our country's freer years, were usually at least eighty acres in size, seventy-eight to seventy-nine acres more than my wife and I wanted. Almost all of that immense expanse is today the fiefdom of a provincial government bureaucracy which abhors the idea of individual ownership of land. Corporate purchase of Crown lands may be accommodated. Corporations, like governments, are bureaucratic institutions and therefore have status. Next to the old sayings that diamonds are a girl's best friend and that gentlemen prefer blondes paste another in your hat: bureaucrats do all their best work in the clinches, provided they clinch with other bureaucrats and not with ordinary folk.

Individuals pose problems for bureaucrats. Individuals fail to fill out the requisite forms in the spaces provided. Even when they do fill them out, they usually get them wrong. Individuals offend against that great, grand, majestic and utterly specious thing called POLICY. Policy is the word bureaucrats use when they substitute illegal activities for legal ones.

I have hung around bureaucrats for about as long as is safe for any man in normal health. I understand their point of view. Their solution to the land problem in B.C. is entirely rational: forbid private ownership of land by various forms of trickery. Even when, as one article in this book details, the trickery is so blatant that the courts deplore it and try to order restitution, it is a passing summer storm and soon forgotten. Policies are stronger than laws. So I leased land instead of buying it. They said that was permissible.

There came another shadow over life in our own country. Laws and regulations began to fall upon Canadians with the persistency of wet February snow. Government agencies bred like blowflies. We reached a condition in this land where law and regulations having the force of law became so numerous that there was no longer any individual who could claim to know more than a few of them, even if helped by lawyers and accountants. Not an acre of Canada could be walked without putting a foot into three or four cowflaps of law, and whether or not you were haled into court for this depended not upon the gravity of the offence but upon a mere administrative decision made by someone you never knew or saw. Clearly it was only a matter of time before everything in Canada was either compulsory or forbidden.

There were ever fewer places left upon the face of the earth where a person might be alone. That is something the Christian Bible warns us against but we haven't much time for the Bible any more. We read regulations instead.

More and more, my wife and I got the impression that we belonged to organizations we had never joined. We gave the leased land back to the Crown and the cabin to a rancher who dismantled it and reassembled it on his own private property, doubtless in contravention of some regional district bylaw. At least it is being used. We still spend a good part of each year in Chilcotin but we use a house trailer and are not readily visible to government officials.

We built our alternate home in Mexico where, just on the far rim of living memory, ordinary people fought a terrible revolution under the slogan "Land And Liberty."

We help to populate a small village which measures one kilometre from side to side and sits on the shore of a vast lagoon, just close enough to the open Pacific for us to hear the surf pounding on the beach which the villagers call The Drum.

The village of Teacapan, state of Sinaloa, did not rate mention in Rand McNally's big, thick Mexican guidebook published in 1971, perhaps because it was isolated from the highway system until causeways were built in the 1960s. North is the resort city of Mazatlán, south the big city of Guadalajara and, not far from Teacapan, somewhere in the modern state of Nayarit whose border lies half a kilometre from our house, is believed to be the original home of the nomadic Aztecs. The Aztecs were the gypsies of this huge nation before becoming its masters.

Although 1250 kilometres south of the U.S. border, this is northern Mexico, traditionally considered frontier country, much as Canadians now view the Northwest Territories and the Yukon.

I have always liked the Territories and the Yukon also. It seems you can exercise the northing instinct in any country.

In this little place, which is far from prosperous and none too clean, we have been privileged to find men, women and children of grace, courtesy and that quality not precisely definable which we call class. We have been reminded that courtesy is more important than wearing socks and that humour can substitute for meat. And these people, like those of Chilcotin, say, "God keep our rulers . . . far away from us."

No doubt the Mexico pieces in this book suffer the fault that some would find with the pieces about Chilcotin and elsewhere. Wherever I may be, I tend, like all writers, to seek out people with characteristics appealing to me and there is then a tendency to apply those characteristics to all the other inhabitants. So I am probably guilty of stereotyping the Mexican people and I am sorry for it. Let it be said in my defence that it is the general mannerisms of a people which first become apparent, particularly when one is groping along in a second language. I know very well that in our village, which is so small that it doesn't have an elected mayor nor even a cast-iron general and horse in the town square, there is not a single stereotype of the Mexican which you could not find contradicted, utterly, by the men and women now living there. They are like people anywhere, infinitely variable and forever unpredictable.

But some qualities—warmth, smile and song—seem to shine through always and I hope they are visible in these few short pieces.

Some things have changed since the articles in this book were first written. But updating material creates new problems, so it seems best to leave them as they are. Readers can only be reminded that we live in an age where you cannot stay in one place, no matter how fast you run. The one constant in our lives is change.

Those who have read *Chilcotin Holiday* may remember my conclusion that no holiday lasts forever. Yet mine continues to this day.

My luck holds.

How Red Lost His Ranch

|||

BIG CREEK—Last Saturday, Red Allison and other friends of the late Ronnie Tomlinson came up to Twilight Ranch and, in the grove of golden poplar where Ronnie's ashes are scattered, they erected a small plaque in his memory.

It's four years since the guy died, which proves that people up here still haven't got a very good handle on that thing called time, but the thought was good.

There are a lot of thoughts about Twilight Ranch, Ronnie Tomlinson, and Red Allison: thoughts of hope, of sadness, and, in the end, with Red, something a trifle noble shining through.

My first note on Red Allison relates to a Williams Lake stampede of about twenty years ago. Red was drunker than fourteen hundred dollars and so was his companion. Fancying they had some disagreement, Red took a roundhouse swing at the chin of his buddy, missed by about a foot and a half, lost his balance, and tried to save himself from falling by grabbing his opponent's belt. The other fellow lost his balance and they both fell into the dust.

Red turned his big, pink, boyish face to the other and snarled: "Why can't you SHTAND UP and FIGHT like a MAN?" Clearly, Red was a man of some distinction, and so it proved.

Over the years he did many things, always well. For quite a few years he ran the general store at Riske Creek in Chilcotin. When the big OK Ranch on the other side of the Fraser River was in absentee ownership, Red was manager, again for many years.

He raised a family and a good reputation but made no great amount of money. He had a little piece of land here, another little piece there. He has a little piece in the Clinton area now.

Also, for a number of years, he was a silent partner in the Twilight Ranch here at Big Creek. Ronnie Tomlinson, a very quiet Englishman from Yorkshire, couldn't raise enough money for a down payment when the place came up for sale. Red came in on shares.

Ronnie proved to be an excellent rancher. The Twilight grew just a bit better, year by year. Fences were renewed. New grazing leases were acquired. Land was cleared. Always it was done a little bit at a time because that's how the money to do it came in, one dollar at a time.

At about the time the Twilight began to look like a model small ranch, Ronnie complained to his cowboy one morning that he felt funny, somehow, and was going to lie down. Twenty minutes later he was dead of a heart problem that he never knew he had.

Since he was a bachelor and clearly had had no thoughts about dying in middle age, people were not surprised when no will was found. So in the normal process of law, the Twilight was sold, Red was paid off for his share, and the balance, a sizable bite out of a million-dollar bill, went to Ronnie's old mother in England.

Red would have dearly loved to have taken over Twilight. It was a ranch just of a size and type for him and his family to run. But a couple of things had happened since he first became a silent partner. Ronnie had repaid Red a fair portion of what he contributed. More, Ronnie had so improved the place, and speculators had driven all ranch prices so high, that it was impossible for Red to raise enough cash to buy Ronnie's share of the place from the estate.

Last fall, three years after Ronnie's death, I ran into Red at a Williams Lake cattle auction where he was buying, selling, and just poking around. It was a shame, I said, that he did not become the owner of the Twilight place, there in the shallow valley of the Bambrick Creek with the green pine hills standing over the yellow grass meadows.

"Oh, then you don't know the rest of the story," he said. He giggled. He is a big man, over six feet, and mostly made of muscle, but he has always had a high-pitched girlish voice and a girlish giggle. He must have had a hard time with both during school days.

No, I knew no more to the story.

Well, Red said, not long ago he got a call from a Williams Lake lawyer. This lawyer had taken over the files of another Williams Lake lawyer who had died, or gone to Heaven, Hell, or the Supreme Court, wherever it is lawyers go when they quit working.

"He had only just got around to going through these cardboard boxes full of the other lawyer's files and what does he find but Ronnie Tomlinson's will. There it is, all signed, sealed, and proper, and it leaves the entire ranch to me."

"What are you going to do, Red?"

"Well, the lawyer said a will is a will and this is a real one. If I went to court, I could overturn everything that had happened and get the Twilight. But of course, I couldn't do that.

"Can you imagine me asking some judge to tell Ronnie's old mother in England that she has got to give all that money back to me? I couldn't possibly do a thing like that."

So he told the lawyer to forget the whole business and let the tail go with the hide. His last tie with Twilight was cut last Saturday when he put the plaque in the poplar grove so men would remember his partner.

Joe's Electric and the Truck That Drove Itself

|||

BIG CREEK—Character shapes companies and the character of Ryan Watt shaped a company here called Joe's Electric, a company that, alas, the world has now lost.

Ryan was a ranch kid, one of a bunch raised at the Breckness ranch in Big Creek, Chilcotin. All the brothers and sisters were different one from another, as usual. Ryan's difference was that he liked to listen rather than to talk and to be unnoticed rather than noticed.

Twenty years ago that characteristic brought him to the attention of the police.

An RCMP constable on a rare visit to Big Creek passed a farm truck that was bustling along the road with nobody driving it. Being a policeman, he was naturally curious and decided to investigate the phenomenon.

When he turned round and followed the truck he thought he could see the head of a small child that barely came above the dashboard to peep through the steering wheel. It was Ryan, age eleven, who was on his way to the one-room Big Creek school.

He had bolted wood blocks to the brake and clutch pedals so his feet would reach them, and except on hard bumps when he sat low in the seat, he was always able to see over the dash to the road.

But when the constable got the truck pulled over, there was still nobody in it. Ryan had slipped out the passenger door and was crouched beside it. "I was terrified," he says now. "There were almost as many Bengal tigers in Chilcotin then as there were policemen."

When the constable came round one side of the truck, Ryan went the opposite way, always keeping the vehicle between them. "I could see which way his boots were turning, looking under the truck," he recalls.

After two full circuits of the truck the pair finally met one another and the policeman was reasonable enough. He just told Ryan not to practise driving on the public highway, and Ryan refrained from saying that was how he and his brother went to school every day.

When he became an electrician and set himself up in business in Williams Lake, Ryan clung to the view that there is no point in bringing yourself to other people's attention needlessly. When his accountant set up Ryan's company, he asked what the name should be.

"Let's say it's my dog's business—call it Joe's Electric," said Ryan, pointing at his Labrador retriever, which was sleeping, as usual.

At that time, as when he drove the driverless truck, he did not foresee how hard anonymity is to achieve in this world. His customers kept asking for Joe. "I would say, 'Well, it's not a good day to see Joe. He was out on the town last night and he's in pretty tough shape today. If you must talk to him, go out in the yard. He's sleeping under the truck.'

"Lots of people would ask why Ryan Watt was signing Joe's Electric cheques. I would always tell them the truth—that he was sitting out in the truck, that he wasn't working today and hadn't worked all week, or that I hadn't seen him since Tuesday."

He could also explain that Joe, although the best sort you could ever hope to meet, the kind you'd be willing to go hunting with, did have his imperfections and that the truth of the matter was he had never learned to read and couldn't even write his own name.

There were, perhaps, those who became puzzled when they demanded and received the full name of Joe of Joe's Electric. It was Gunanoot's Joe of Terror.

In time, Joe died, as dogs do. Ryan got another dog, a springer spaniel. It was good at busting grouse out of heavy cover but,

Ryan says, it didn't have the temperament for business. It lacked the solidity, the stability of the Labrador.

Joe's Electric disappeared from the Williams Lake yellow pages. Ryan now helps run a motorcycle agency with the ordinary, everyday, and uninspiring name Williams Lake Honda.

Lazy, You Say? The Future Holds Riches or Fame

||||

BIG CREEK—For more than a week it was known to all that Morgan was entered in the speechmaking contest at the 4-H Club meeting at the TH Ranch. Everybody knew because his mother nagged him so much about it.

"Morgan, don't forget you're in the 4-H speech contest."

"Oh, Mom."

"Have you started it?"

"I haven't had time."

"You had time to walk around with the .22 looking for grouse."

"I'll get it done."

"What's your subject?"

"I'll think of something."

"Mor-gan!"

It was enough to make a visitor reflect that most mothers and most sons are the same, generation by generation.

To Morgan's mother, life is a fairly serious business. She was left a grass widow some years ago and has raised Morgan and his brother by herself. She has a few beef cows and a horse for cowboying. The boys have saddle horses to ride to school. They live in an old log cabin in which the sills have rotted so that the floors wave enough to make some people seasick walking across them.

In addition to running the district's smallest ranch, the mother keeps a pig to slaughter for winter food and tends chickens and a goat. She works outside, as it is said. She is janitor of the one-room schoolhouse. She cooks for loggers and goes as cook on trail

rides. No work seems too tough for her. She has even taken con-
tracts to creosote railway ties, which is about as miserable a job
as can be devised.

Morgan, whom I have observed over several years, has been
known to avoid work, although he invents work for himself of a
rather arresting nature. Two years ago, when he was eleven, he
decided that what the one-room school needed was a newspaper.
He produced one, monthly, for a school term.

On the front page he proclaimed his publishing policy:

!AN EXCITING, HAPPY, GORY NEWSPAPER!

I have not heard the newspaper business described so suc-
cinctly by many professional editors, who would like to have said
it that way.

Morgan reported therein all that happened in Big Creek school
and, when that wasn't much, he made up stories.

I was unable to hear him at the 4-H public speaking competition. On that day it chanced that I had a previous engagement to
meet some blue grouse on the sidehills of the Chilcotin River.
That night, however, I went to Morgan's home. He was in bed,
no doubt thinking of great things he was going to do someday. I
talked to his mother.

"Morgan makes me so angry," she said. "Friday night he
finally decided he was going to talk about chicken raising. He
wrote about ten words and then went off to play. This morning he
finally got the thing finished just three minutes before we had to
leave in the car for the TH."

"So he did not do well?"

"That's what makes me so angry. He won."

Ah dear, the old Protestant work ethic, alive and causing
trouble in the ranch country.

"He got up in front of everybody so damn calm. Since people
were talking to each other, he held off speaking. He went: 'Aruk
tuk tuk tuk.' Well, everybody went silent and from then on he
couldn't say anything wrong at that meeting, even though all the
stuff in his speech he'd cribbed out of the encyclopedia."

"Tell me, did anybody go to the 4-H meeting to learn about
raising chickens?"

"Well, no. We all know more about it than he does."

"Was there anybody there who was nervous about whether the kids would be able to speak or not?"

"Sure. Everybody was. It's a relief to see any kid get through the thing. Public speaking is a strain on the audience as well as the kids."

"Yes, except Morgan, who was at ease and put everybody else at ease?"

"Well," she said, "I s'pose you could say that."

"And when he was through, nobody remembered exactly what he had said but they were sure he had said something worthwhile?"

"Yes. But . . ."

"But me no buts. Let us assume, for the sake of argument, that your son is lazy, impulsive, given to procrastination, and sometimes flighty in the head. Did you not know that practically everybody in the newspaper business, worldwide, is like that?"

"You mean he might make a newspaperman?"

"Well, I don't think he's going to be a nuclear physicist or a brain surgeon, but yes, he might become famous as a newspaperman or, if he turns out bone lazy, even more famous as a TV anchorman on one of the big network news shows."

"And what if that doesn't happen?"

"If that doesn't come to pass, given his ability to make public speeches which warm an audience without informing them about anything, he could become a prime minister of Canada. That isn't a steady job and it doesn't pay as well as TV work, but it would be better than his hanging around pool halls."

She sniffed in the way women sometimes do when they wish a conversation to end.

Perce's Rubber Worm

|||

ANAHIM LAKE—Every time an election is called I think about Perce Hance and the rubber worm.

All the Hances of Hanceville were gentlemanly except for a couple of lady Hances who were ladylike. The original Chilcotin Hance, Tom, came from the American South, where manners rank higher than money on the social scale. His several sons and daughter were taught that once you abandoned good manners you had lost any argument, no matter how good your position had been to start with.

Percy, eldest of the family, first white child born west of the Fraser River, held tenaciously to that view. Perce never killed anybody or, so far as I know, ever hit anybody particularly hard. However, if Perce Hance intended to kill you, he was the kind of man who would first make a small bow and present you with an Easter lily in prime condition to hold in your left hand before he shot you.

One night at the old TH Ranch, when night's candles were burning out and the whiskey running low, Marian Witte asked if anyone would care for food and Perce said well, many thanks, and might it be possible for him to have just one small sandwich.

She made him a roast beef sandwich in the kitchen. Somebody I shall not identify, except to say that it was not me, went to a fishing tackle box, removed a long rubber worm, and put it in the sandwich. By the time Perce got his sandwich, several people in the room knew it had a gutta-percha lining and there was high expectancy.

Perce took a bite and became thoughtful. He bit again. He bit as hard as a man with store teeth top and bottom can bite.

There was a sound like a sharp string breaking. Perce chewed and swallowed that first bite.

It was the moment to shout "Happy April Ferce, Perce." Nobody did. He spoke first.

"Exactly what I wanted," he said. "There is nothing tastier than a good beef sandwich."

All impulses to cheers or laughter died away and were replaced by a broad dismay. Should he be warned? Was there anything poisonous about artificial fishworms, coloured purple, as sold by Army & Navy in Vancouver?

Anything that could have been said should have been said immediately, and since it was not said there remained only general apprehension.

Perce slowly, gamely, ate the whole sandwich. A bounce at a time, as someone said later.

He declined the offer of another beef sandwich. The first, he said, had been perfect. He died, many years later, without knowing about the rubber worm.

Now of course some people will say, what has this got to do with elections?

Well, it has a lot to do with elections.

After the eating of the rubber worm there was a lot of silence lying around that room, and somebody offered up a political story. It contained, he said, everything that anybody need ever know about the art of politics and it all happened one hot summer's day on Becher's Prairie, just up the road a piece.

"From Becher House they could see this truck coming across the range. It would run maybe a hundred, two hundred yards. Then it would stop. The driver would get out with a piece of two-by-four in his hand. He would slam the two-by-four on the sides of the truck box. Then he would run back to the cab and drive another hundred yards or so before he did it again.

"When he got to Becher House somebody said, 'Could you tell us exactly what is going on?'

"The driver said: 'Yes. It's very simple. This is a one-ton truck. I am packing two tons of canaries in it. I have got to keep at least half of them flying all the time."

Now you, too, understand all about politics. Keep at least half of the people up in the air all the time. And you understand why every time an election writ drops I think about Perce Hance and a rubber worm.

Kitchen Midden

|||

My heart is in Chilcotin but I left my liver at the Lakeview Hotel.—Old Cariboo saying, author unknown

WILLIAMS LAKE—Archaeologists dig up what are called kitchen middens to discover the shape of life in societies of long ago. They find broken household implements, knives, beads, and all the bits and pieces that formed a community's life.

It is in this sense that Randy Brunner's collection of notes from the night clerks of the Lakeview Hotel should be viewed. The notes are a discovery, one that our province may well wish to preserve, as we preserve old Indian middens. But for the treasure you must sift tons of waste.

Randy, who died in 1981, was owner and manager of the Lakeview from 1950 to 1975. The old hotel is itself a monument. It was built in the 1890s and was extended a couple of times since. It is now being renovated again. At the time these notes were entered it was the old, familiar, rambling place, a bit cluttered, often infested with mice and sometimes cockroaches. It was and is a watering hole for ranchers, cowboys, and Indians out of Chilcotin and other parts of the Back of Beyond.

The night clerks' notes were made on spiral stenographer's notepads. The handwriting of several staff people is to be found. Randy and his clerks made the notebooks a central information depot. Therein they exchanged jokes, gossip, and the tedious details of broken Coke machines, missing linens, and that ever-present phenomenon of hotel operation, the india-rubber cheque.

"When M. comes in ask if he needs a room for Stampede as he is a Regular." Another staffer writes: "A regular something, alright."

"Anita. Young punks were very good Friday so guess they had to make up for it Saturday. Foam pillows in 104 and 105 need recovering."

"If Polly B. is out of her suite don't let her son have the key. He has too many friends."

"Just read your note about Duane W. not having any water in his room. After 48 hours at Guides' Convention guess he had a fire to put out."

"Aussie hears there is a girl serving drinks at the Chilcotin Inn. What will they do next there?" (This, a notation from the year 1968, not 1908. How fast some of our ideas changed!)

The Pacific Great Eastern morning train couldn't leave the station because the crew at the Lakeview didn't get wake-up calls.

The café refused to give a second cup of coffee free to a regular guest. He knows Randy will want to know of this atrocity. John W. in 204 is more plaintive than bellicose . . . "doesn't mind mice in the room but objects when they crawl into bed with him."

"114 took his 'wife' up. I peeled the bark off him. He said 'We've been married for 17 years.' I said 'Congratulations, now get her the hell out of here.' " (Two days later, 114 thanks the clerk for his discriminating kindness and this too goes into the record.)

"Watch 218. Heavy drinker AND smoker."

Alcohol runs all through the narrative. Often it's funny but the sad and the sordid aspects of the drug are there too. "T. in 221 has not come in yet. Little girl still there. Suggest you check for her breakfast, etc."

The next note, in other handwriting: "Girls are looking after T's daughter but if he asks DON'T tell him what room they're in as he is gassed."

A day later: "T. rather pugnatious [sic] at desk so told him what I thought of his neglect of child. Reminded him of his debt to office staff for feeding the child etc."

There are guests who are loved. Money is loaned to them, errands are run, phone calls made, wives pacified. There are others whose arrival is regarded much as Vienna anticipated the arrival of the Turkish army.

One such is John P. of Chilcotin who throws his empty bottles out the window and narrowly misses pedestrians. He can't be broken of the habit but he must be taken in because his category is a Regular. A Regular is something like a king or a pope. You can't just boot his ass out onto the street.

There is an exchange of notes as to whether a change of the moon is the main factor influencing the behaviour of hotel guests.

The vast, the overwhelming bulk of the notes in the spiral-lock pads are, like fragments in a kitchen midden, the multitudinous chores of housekeeping, the ceaseless lament of a mother picking up after the members of a vast, careless, irresponsible, charming, and occasionally impossible family. Ironing, burned-out lights, torn linen, and bathrooms that didn't get cleaned; messages, money for safekeeping, slow pays, plugged toilets, worn carpets, noise, underage girls, lost keys, the heat, the cold, the drafts, and windows that won't open.

"211 tried to talk me into thinking the Communist government in U.S.S.R. is better than our capitalist gov. Why don't people who think Russia is so good go there?" (Other handwriting) "They're too lazy, Russians are too smart to let them in."

Set beside Randy Brunner's twenty kilos of notebooks, can the records of the Pearson, Trudeau, or Clark cabinet meetings serve as well to document the realities of our age? Not as far as Williams Lake is concerned they can't.

The Corporate Beef Drive

|||

A long time ago, when I was more stupid, I learned almost everything about the economics of the beef industry from my friend Duane Witte. We were moving his cattle from the spring grass in the valley of the Chilcotin River to his summer range.

He ran a cow-calf outfit. Soon after our little drive, much of the beef industry shifted to farm and feedlot operations and, as we all know, ever since then things have got more and more wonderful until finally we got to where we are now. But I speak of an old-fashioned open-range operation, back in the days when earth was young—about 1975.

Down in the valley of the Chilcotin that year the whole operation of moving his cattle came to depend on the health and spirit of one old grade Hereford cow. She had aborted and been discovered prostrated on a narrow bench, two hundred metres up from the river, five hundred metres down from the cow camp. The trail to her was about as steep as a pitched roof on a ski lodge.

Two or three times a day we would clamber down that slope on our saddle horses. We carried a pail of water, a sack of grain, and a rifle. The plan was that if she looked sicker, Duane would shoot her and we would get on with the drive. If she showed any cheerfulness we would feed her, water her, give her some Dr. Bell's and lift her to her feet for a few minutes.

Somehow, to Duane, she always looked cheerful.

To get her on her feet he and I would work the front end and his cowboy, Bobbie Brush, would crank the tail to get her hind end up. To anyone not experienced in getting a cow in this condition on her feet the advice is, never take the south end of the job. Bobbie would stand there, his Levis streaming, and from time to time he would say, plaintively, "I should have been a brain surgeon, like Mother wanted."

After three days the cow became infected with some of Duane's optimism, so the beef drive proceeded from Spring Turnout to his summer range at Teepee Heart Ranch in Big Creek. Even during the drive, Duane made two seventy-five-kilometre round trips to the Turnout to check on her condition and stopped only because she eventually walked off. It turned out later that she took up with a Gang Ranch bull on the nearby range. She had obviously forgotten what had given her all her trouble in the first place.

To get a grasp of the economics of this operation I applied to Duane's wife, Marian. Why days of delay and wear and tear on trucks and men when an eleven-cent bullet could have been used?

"No problem," she said. "It just means that when we sell her we will have to get four times as much as has ever been paid for a cow at a Williams Lake auction. That's all. Someday, if you bite into that cow at McDonald's, just remember you are eating twenty-dollar-a-pound beef."

If they ever got that price I never heard of it. My suspicion is that the sick cow was one of the reasons that Duane never drove BMWs or had movie stars for mistresses.

You may well ask what would be the use of offering advice to Duane about cash flow and such matters. He was a typical rancher and would doubtless give the classic response: "Hell, man, I don't need good advice. I am not running this outfit half as good as I already know how to."

But it may be suggested that this account of an overoptimistic rancher and his cow should not be left here. It could help our understanding of the world if we take a look at how other people might have handled the cow.

In my life I have had much contact with bureaucracies. They usually win while I lose, so they must be smarter than me.

How would a big government bureaucracy or the bureaucracy of any large private corporation handle the cow on the sidehill?

Consider first how many divisions would have to be deployed.

There would be Medical (the cow was sick), Accountancy (who else to keep track of overtime?), and Public Information to keep the Greenpeace people away; also Personnel (the union shop steward would almost certainly show up), the Agricultural Department (Crown grazing land was involved), and Support Services for tents, cookhouses, first-aid stations, mobile repair shops, FAX machines, and separate but equal bathroom facilities for female staff.

A task force would be formed.

There would be any God's amount of planning, something in which they say the rest of us are lamentably deficient, and no prairie blizzard could match the amount of paper filling the sky.

One great misfortune, and a very common one, might complicate matters. If it turned out that two vice-presidents or two deputy ministers had an almost equal involvement in the project, all planning, all activity would come to a halt while the two people fought out the important battle—who was to be kept off whose turf?

In the end, a turf battle is usually referred upstairs, to a capital city such as Victoria or Ottawa or, in the case of private industry, to a corporate headquarters in Toronto or New York. The mails, it will be recalled, don't move as rapidly now as in the nineteenth century and the delay is becoming as long as an arctic winter.

As any normal person can perceive, by the time the rescue convoy hits the road the cow is long dead. But some normal people still don't perceive that in a bureaucratic operation, this makes no difference whatsoever. Forms have been made and signed, flow charts have been drawn, a system and a policy have been put in place. If these function as expected, the operation will be successful and its original purpose, if the original purpose can be remembered by anyone, will be a trivial detail.

Out in the ill-organized world of ranchers, farmers, fishermen, small businessmen and the other rabble of society there are an extraordinary number of people who cannot grasp one simple truth—in a big operation it is not what you accomplish that counts but how extensively you have organized your activities.

People who don't recognize this because of purposeful obtuseness deserve all the indignities and costs which big government and big business heap upon them.

Of course, despite all the committee meetings, the great cow rescue operation would probably not proceed according to plan. As one of the B.C. government's most highly paid servants once cheerfully assured me, "Anything that can go wrong will go wrong."

If losses are under half a million dollars, they can probably be hidden under Miscellaneous in the annual report. However, at higher figures it may be necessary to form a task force or a royal commission to examine the matter and to ensure that the innocent are punished and the guilty promoted.

All things considered, I prefer Duane's way.

He lost on the cow rescue operation but it was his loss, not mine. When big business or big government loses money, I am expected to cough up money so that profits and executive salaries are safeguarded. The more the big outfits lose, the higher my taxes and the prices of everything I buy.

Also, it is worth mentioning that doing it Duane's way meant there was one more cow in the world than there would otherwise have been, and that cannot be entirely bad.

Longhorns, Again, at the Oldest Ranch

|||

ALKALI LAKE—Here on the oldest ranch in Canada, under a frosty late autumn sunset which is red as a russet apple, all the air of the valley is shaken by the lamentations of 330 cows who have been separated from their calves, who have just been weaned. Such loud melancholy may have attended the expulsion of the ten tribes of Israel. The calves also wail about it.

In our time there is no such mourning except that of captains of industry who find their corporations suddenly deprived of government welfare payments. Industrialists, like beef calves, lament when asked to stand on their own feet and seek their own nourishment.

Fourteen hundred calves this year, Doug Mervyn says. That is 500 more than when he bought Alkali Lake Ranch a little more than nine years ago.

Doug does not wish to be known as a gentleman rancher. He wants the place to be a model ranch, which means a paying proposition. He needs that. He paid $2½ million for the Alkali. Later this evening, we will examine one of the old deeds which shows 160 prime acres of the home place selling to one of the original owners for a five-dollar bill.

We walk up to the big house built by a previous owner (fourteen bedrooms, eight bathrooms), under the linden trees, imported from Europe, and talk about this historic piece of ground.

The name itself puzzles many. There is a lake near the big house called Alkali Lake but it is not and never has been an alkali lake. Turns out the first settler called this Paradise Valley. Men walking the trail to the Cariboo goldfields remembered it better by the prominent white alkali scar on the valley's northern face and called it Alkali Valley. In time the name transferred to the lake and to the ranch.

Herman Otto Bowe, a Frisian from Helgoland who had mined in California and at Barkerville, preempted land here on March 19, 1863, and the next year drove 500 head of Texas longhorn up from the Oregon territory to start the ranch.

This apparently makes it the oldest ranch in Canada. Plenty of farmers kept cattle for beef long before that but as parts of farm operations. Of the true, open-range cattle ranch, this one is rated as the original. It is at least a more probable claim than that the Gang Ranch is the biggest ranch in the world. You could drop twenty Gang Ranches into some of the northern Australian ranches and not be able to find them.

Herman Bowe came first; Henry Bowe, his son, second. C. W. Wynn-Johnson bought the Alkali in 1909 and sold in 1939 to Mario von Riedemann. Mario died and was succeeded by his son Martin Riedemann, who died of hypothermia after upsetting in the lake during a Halloween fireworks party.

In 1976, Doug and Marie Mervyn had just sold their big ski operation outside Kelowna. They bought and moved into the big house that had been built in the time of Mario, a handsome place but depressingly large, says Marie, particularly with three of the four children grown and gone.

Although Doug had herded sheep for a year, when young and footloose, he did not know much about ranching. "What I had and what I kept was the Riedemann's manager, Bronc Twan. He has a few cowboys, according to the season, but not many any more. Although we still do have a cowboy bunkhouse on this place."

Doug and Marie both cowboy and do all the many manners of work available for using up your time on a ranch. The day, it is said, is usually done before Doug is.

The surprise of the evening's conversation is to discover history making a neat, circular turn here on the Alkali. Doug Mervyn, who after nine years has developed some firm ideas of his own, is making a partial return to the Texas longhorn stock of the last century. His cows are Hereford, with some of the exotic Simmental, but most of his bulls are longhorn.

"There's more than one reason. The shoulders are smaller and the cows give birth easier. We used to have twenty to thirty Caesarean births a year. Last year we didn't have one. The meat is leaner. I think the animals are hardier. After all, the longhorn developed here on this continent out of feral Spanish cattle."

It is Doug's conviction that most cattlemen have lost touch with their customers. They are wedded to the idea of blocky whitefaces, larded with fat. "But the customer doesn't want fat anymore. He wants lean meat."

In Wyoming, he says, ranchers on an experimental program increased sales by more than 50 per cent by raising meat called Wyoming Lean, twenty-two to twenty-four months old, exclusively grass-fed.

The beef industry has got to stop producing six billion pounds of unwanted fat every year, says the newest owner of the oldest ranch. Next morning the animals are still bawling.

"Another two days and they'll quit complaining," says Doug. *There* is a difference from corporation executives. If cut off from a government subsidy, their squawling has only begun at the end of three days.

The Land Where Diogenes Put Out His Lantern

|||

ALEXIS CREEK—A few reports from Chilcotin, the country where Diogenes finally put out his lantern . . .

The Downwind Tracker's wife reports on winter in Big Creek:

"We set off with the milk cow to take her to the bull to be bred. The Downwind Tracker was on the tractor. He likes to be driver. He dragged the wagon which had three bound bales of hay and me on it. At the end of a long rope was the Jersey.

"She came along all right at first but about halfway there she remembered how much trouble she'd got into with bulls before and started slewing around. We had a long march.

"Five minutes after meeting the bull she decided he wasn't her type and beat a trail for the home place with him in pursuit. I can't blame her in a way—he is big and nasty and needlessly masculine.

"When we returned from feeding the bull had her up against the hay shed. The Downwind Tracker drove the tractor right in between them and the Jersey went galloping off into three-foot snowdrifts.

"The Downwind Tracker said, 'Catch her, catch her.' I started plowing through the snow. My husband, still sitting on the tractor, then hollers, 'Run, before he beats you to her.'

"We didn't talk much to one another at dinnertime."

|||

Misfortune overtook the Plummers of Deer Creek. They are starting a ranch of their own, based on the Wilson Meadow, and had skidded a 15×20 log cabin thirty miles to there.

Left empty, it burned to the ground with all its few contents, uninsured, of course, like everything else in the country.

The police were curious. "Mr. Plummer," they said, "do you have any enemies? Is there somebody who holds a grudge against you?"

Wayne Plummer, a quiet, slow-spoken man, thought awhile and then said, "Only the government."

| | |

The *Globe and Mail,* which collects statistics, reports that the number of full-time farmers in Canada has now dropped to 90,000, while the number of full-time civil servants in the various governments' agricultural departments, which are devoted to looking after farmers, has reached 18,000.

There is now one person writing memorandums for every five people forking the raw manure.

The *Economist* magazine, examining Russia's agriculture, finds that in that country's agricultural industry one person in three is a government employee. This shows how advanced Communists are in planning.

Given time, in both nations the number of bureaucrats will exceed the number of farmers. There will come a day when the entire industry is composed of bureaucrats and nobody is left to grow spuds, raise beef, watch the northern lights at calving time or otherwise complicate flow charts which will, by then, have been finally perfected.

| | |

In Chilcotin when a woman has twins there are four of them.

| | |

The Chilcotin has further contributed to the expansion of the English language as follows:

Chilcotin dragline: a shovel

Chilcotin overdrive: coasting downhill in neutral

Chilcotin credit card: a gas siphon hose

Chilcotin holiday: leaving home for several days with no more provisions than one horse, one rifle and one shaker of salt

Chilcotin cheque: cash

Chilcotin sandwich: a shot of whiskey and a dry, folded napkin, provided in establishments whose liquor licence forbids serving alcoholic beverages except with meals

Chilcotin socket wrench set: a pair of slip joint pliers

Chilcotin turkey: a river-run salmon which has been illegally dip-netted by a white or legally netted by an Indian and then illegally sold to a white; the flavour comes from the illegality

| | |

Further samples of the English language as it is booted around in Chilcotin:

Description of a truly rank horse: "I would know that horse again if I met him as hide on a pair of boots in Halifax."

A rodeo cowboy telling how he was thrown by a great bucking horse: "I had never before seen the stampede grounds from that altitude."

About another ornery shitter: "He was one of them horses it takes you a long time to get on him but scantly any time to get off him."

Disbelief for Fun and Profit

||||

Just luck, probably, but it was my luck: I learned to disbelieve things. There is nothing better for fun and profit than disbelief.

It began when I was just old enough to seed and cultivate my first adult paranoias. The idea of vitamins had just burst from somebody's brow. A vitamin C pill a day kept scurvy away, but barely. Without a close count on their vitamin intake man and boy were hell-bent for death or lunacy.

As with many things, I did not exactly disbelieve in vitamins. I just disbelieved in almost everything that people said about vitamins.

Also I had access to heretical books, such as John Steinbeck's *Cannery Row*. Steinbeck wrote of the Spanish-American woman who fed her children nothing but vitamin-free refried beans. They thrived, as do so many who reject expert advice.

Germs, microbes, and bacteria had a lurid appeal some years ago. With a slide rule one could calculate that a single pinprick could admit organisms that in their rapid breeding would utterly consume the body. Six were enough, for starters, to overwhelm a city the size of Toronto.

Today medical researchers say that perhaps the creation of disease resistance within the human body is more important than counting how many germs can dance on a housefly's moustache. I didn't need a white coat to come to that conclusion. I arrived at it by the simple process of disbelief.

Disbelief saved me much anguish during the Vietnam war.

When the time came that the U.S. army's claim of enemy casualties had exceeded the number of soldiers in the enemy's army I stopped reading Pentagon press releases. Years later General Haig was to lose a libel suit against a TV network that accused him of complicity in misleading the American people. I was twenty years ahead of the U.S. courts. Disbelief, nothing more.

Once you get the trick of disbelieving it is a comfort better than whiskey, and cheaper.

Take those Communist poison gas attacks in Vietnam. Yellow Rain, it was called.

I wasted not one second of my life believing in Yellow Rain. There could be no better unwasting. It turns out now that the Yellow Rain was only bumblebee doodoo. For me there is no agonizing reappraisal. I arrived at the same point by the easy method of disbelief.

In the same way, I now enjoy disbelief in acid rain.

I do not believe the ozone layer in the stratosphere is decreasing and I do not believe the carbon dioxide layer is increasing. I just barely believe in the stratosphere.

I disbelieve almost all the endangered species reports. Maybe the peregrine falcon is endangered in New York City, but so are the people in New York City. The bison is endangered, but only on the prairies, and I trust he will continue endangered there. The spectacle of forty million buffalo treading down the wheat is not appealing.

Also, it's worth noting that people who believe in endangered species almost always believe they have the latest disease and want to talk about it. If they would try some disbelief they would find they had more time for dipping candles.

I do not believe that bankers secretly run the world. Bankers can't run banks.

I do not believe the Bolsheviki are going to conquer us. They have not learned to feed themselves yet.

When I go abroad, disbelief serves me equally well.

At our village in Mexico it is well known that eating watermelon when you have a cold will bring on pneumonia and that a cut will not heal if you persist in eating pork. A disbeliever like me recognizes those as the same old stories the medical profession at home is passing out. You ignore them and keep on enjoying chops and watermelon desserts.

Should one, then, try to live with no beliefs?

Never. It would be like living without love.

The reason for developing disbelief is to leave room for some beliefs worth having. By my abstinence from some of the popular beliefs listed above I was able to indulge in beliefs in other things.

I believe that dogs can laugh. I believe in the nobility of some animals. I believe in the colour of earth as seen from the moon. I believe in Mark Twain, pretty girls, wise grandfathers, and the way of the eagle in the air.

I believe in family. I believe in my country. I sometimes believe that I will live forever, which does no harm. If it proves wrong it won't much matter to me when I find out.

I could never have enjoyed such happy beliefs if I had stuffed my worry bag with beliefs that other people said I had a duty to hold.

No matter how few beliefs you hold, chuck a few overboard. You will be happier. So will the people around you.

Mother's Story

|||

"Tell me," said my wife, "is Natalie a physically attractive woman?"

"Well, she does have a tendency to steam up a man's glasses."

"Now that's funny. I like her a lot, but to me she seems downright homely."

"Maybe she is homely, now that you mention it, but there is something about her . . ."

"What puzzles me even more, Natalie doesn't have any feeling she got shortchanged in the looks department at all. She has that attitude of 'Look, it's me, you lucky guys.' "

"Lucky Natalie," I said, "because if she believes that, at least half of the men she meets will believe it also. She will be what she chooses to be, a beauty."

My wife asked what I knew about such matters and I said that I knew my mother.

My mother spent most of her life convinced that she was an ugly duckling and that she could never have become a swan. She joked about it a lot. She said she was the spitting image of Eleanor Roosevelt.

She used to tell, rather gaily, about a dream she had once in which she entered a beauty contest and the judges all collapsed into hysterical laughter and they had to be passed out over the heads of the audience to the great outdoors where they could recover in the fresh air.

As a kid I didn't pay much attention to whether or not my

mother considered herself attractive. She was Mother, what else mattered?

However, when I grew older I realized that my mother had slightly crippled herself with that ugly-duckling notion.

In Chicago, the Powers modelling agency had suggested to Mother that she might do rather well for herself and her family, financially, by becoming a Powers model. She didn't try, of course.

Partly this was because of the attitude of my father, who was outraged at the thought of his wife modelling clothes in front of strangers. He was old-style French-Canadian. However, in part Mother did not become a Powers model because she believed she would look ridiculous among those long-stemmed beauties. Somebody, surely, was making jokes.

Now, what might the facts be?

No son can be a good judge but, standing well back, looking at it all with what I like to think is a clinical eye, she ranked about 8 or 8½ on the scale of 1 to 10. She had a superb figure, as the Powers agency noted. Her hair was auburn, thick, long, and glossy, and the sun glinted off it even when there wasn't any sun. She had bright blue eyes and a smile that lit up the sky for miles around her.

What had happened to my mother was that she spent her childhood and adolescence among some improbably beautiful cousins. Those cousins, as it chanced, were the model young men and women of the Edwardian age. Every girl was a Gibson Girl and every boy looked like Edward VIII later looked. On the scale of one to ten the Chisholm cousins ranked 9¾.

Only late in her life did my mother get some understanding of this.

"You know, I wasn't *really* all that plain, was I?" she said one day.

"You were never plain, Mother. You had a figure and a smile and a personality that dazzled people."

"Isn't it strange," she said. "Here I am, an old woman with arthritis and a bent back, and I've only just now understood that I had no reason whatever to be apologetic about my appearance."

When my elder daughter was married she put a small, sepia-tone photo of Mother on a table at the entrance to the reception room. It had been taken when Mother graduated from college in 1917. It is an old, faded photograph, but you can see the eyes, the mounds of shining hair, the slope of her white neck.

Small though it was, the wedding guests were arrested by that photo. What a beautiful young woman, they said, how graceful she is. But Mother was no longer alive to hear them.

The Education of Fly

|||

HANCEVILLE—The instructions are to treat her like a Jehovah's Witness at the door of a Sunday morning. No need to get violent, but be hostile. "If you have to, throw rocks at her and miss."

This isn't all that easy if you like border collies, but there was no arguing about it. The next four days were to be the start of her formal education in herding cows, and all her attention as well as her affection had to be focussed on the cowboy who owned her.

So, although she was only seven months old and by nature friendly and playful in the way of adolescents, the little dog named Fly learned, from a few rebuffs, that she did not have another friend up on Fire Creek summer range.

From the first day she had eyes for no one except her master. By the fourth day she was developing also an eye for the cattle to be herded, which is quite a short time even for a breed as bright as the border collie.

In the educational process we were to observe, cowboy and cow dog start with one main advantage. Both have the identical instinct to make cattle move from where they are to some other place where they had not, of their own accord, thought of going.

It is an advantage that this shaggy little twelve-kilo dog, whose ancestors came from Scotland, shares with the Scots a passion for education. It likes to learn.

There are disadvantages also. Despite what the anthropomor-phists suggest, dogs do not understand English or any other language. A dog cannot read words or understand a diagram. Whether it has the capacity to reason is debatable.

Fly's first lesson is to push cows that are drifting left of the line of drive back where they should be, in front of the horsemen. This cowboy's command to go left is "Way Out."

On the first day, the cowboy rides left herself as she gives the command. The dog, which had already learned to follow the human, follows this command. Soon the dog's mind takes the extra step; it runs out left on the command "Way Out" without the owner leading or following.

From this beginning, other commands are jointed on, like sections of a fishing pole, the dog's mind absorbing one section at a time.

One thing that's necessary is to train her to turn the furthest cow back into the line of drive. Her natural inclination is to turn back the first cow she reaches but, by doing so, she will often drive two or more even more distant cows further into the jack pines.

This is accomplished fairly easily by the owner repeating "Way Back" as she comes to the first stray, "Way Back" again at the second, and finally, with a subtle change of inflection, the command "Bring Her Back" at the furthest animal.

Fly gets hung up on the command for retrieving strays from the right side of the line.

The cowboy begins using the command "Come By." When she does, Fly stops, peers at her, even cocks her head to one side in puzzlement, like the old advertisement of a fox terrier listening to His Master's Voice on the gramophone.

The answer, it seems, is that "Come By" is too much the same as the command she used to summon the dog, "Come." So "Come By" is discarded and "Over" used instead.

Again, there having been a change in a command, the little dog is puzzled, but she hesitates only twice. Thereafter she knows "Over" as the order to go right.

How some other commands are transmitted remains puzzling to an observer. When Fly starts to move a cow and is stopped by the order "Leave Her Alone," how is it that she first understands what that means?

Probably it is tone of voice. Something reminds her of negative orders back at the ranch when she was younger. But it is a strange process, this communication between human and dog, and one is powerfully tempted to believe in telepathy.

Or does it all come under the word intelligence?

Wise men don't take intelligence tests among humans too seriously and testing intelligence among the other animals is an even more dubious exercise. However, like gossip, we all take part at one time or another.

Those who engage in such exercise rank the terriers and other vermin killers low on an intelligence scale, since they do no more than run out for prey and kill it. Hunting breeds are higher, the retrievers who run out to bring game back alive or dead to the handler and, above the retrievers, the pointers who direct the hunter to the game while keeping the birds still for his approach. Highest of all in this rating system are border collies and other sheep and cattle dogs who herd other animals.

True?

Who knows? Not thee, brother, nor me.

What can be said of this trip is that by the end of only three days of roundup, Fly has learned an astonishing amount. She shows a clear understanding of the riders' purpose, which is to move cows and bulls in a line ahead without losing any to right or left; also to move them slowly, so that they do not burn off their fat, but not as slowly as the ponderous old bulls would prefer.

To hurry any animal, or to move a stubborn one, Fly has learned the command "Bite 'im." To avoid getting kicked, she should nip the animal just above the hoof. Fly, however, nips higher on the hock and must someday learn, perhaps the hard way, that this is not the place to bite 'im.

Fly also needs courage.

Sooner or later a cow or bull will turn and defy her nipping. Then this mite of a dog must have the courage to throw herself at the face of this monstrously large animal and if necessary nip it on the nose to turn it. However, on this roundup, that test does not present itself to her.

When four days of riding end, Fly has left her childhood and adolescence. She is more reserved, more confident, and much,

much more knowledgeable. She has even begun to develop what is called "eye."

Eye is a communication, not between dog and master, but between dog and cow, a look which conveys to the beef animal that she should abandon her thought of thrashing away into the timber because the dog has anticipated the thought.

Not once in four days does the master find it necessary to strike the dog. Only rarely is Fly scolded.

Finally it is worth noting that Fly was a happy dog.

Dogs are not happiest when sleeping in the sun with full bellies. They are happiest when doing the work they were intended to do. The same goes for humans, and for cowboys who are, as is well known, part human.

Man, Dog and Gun
in the Morning
|||

ALEXIS CREEK—This Monday morning, while it is still dark and cold, the young Chesapeake Bay retriever and I will drive to the duck marsh and shove off in the canoe through shore ice that is thin as an eggshell.

It is possibly the finest moment of the whole hunt, because everything is in our imagination, all is anticipation. As the Chinese say, it is better to travel with hope than to arrive.

The Chesapeake's excitement began building the moment I picked up the old shotgun. Picked it up not on this morning but days ago, down at home in the Fraser Valley.

It is strange how dogs' senses operate. He will sleep unconcerned, giving me no more than the lift of an eyelid, when I dress with a shirt and tie for city wear. But when I pull out the old familiar clothes for hunting, when I start rummaging in the garage for the decoy sack and fiddling with the roof rack and the canoe, his entire attitude changes. He will be underfoot every day, all day, not even excluding sitting in wait for me outside the bathroom door when I seek privacy there.

At such times I would call him a thoroughgoing nuisance, except that he is no crazier about bird shooting than I am.

On Monday morning he will almost certainly anticipate the alarm clock by about five minutes and wake me in my Pioneer down bag by punching me with his nose.

The only touch of sadness Monday will be leaving his mother, old Meg. She will also awaken and be just as excited as the young dog. But she is twelve, very old for a hunting dog, the waters of autumn are too cold for her now, and she is too stiff to climb back into the canoe with a bird in her mouth. So we will leave her to her dreams, which she will shortly resume, there being little except sleep to her life now. Possibly before this duck season ends I can arrange one more retrieve for her on a warm afternoon in calm waters.

In life's coldest hour, the hour before the dawn, the dog Chilco and I will drift down the slow creek that winds through our marsh and hear it murmuring as it rouses itself to a new day. Perched at the bow, he will startle each time a mallard, still hidden by darkness, talks in the weeds. On the other hand, the gabble of coots will not interest him.

Coots are legal game, but we don't shoot them when mallards can be had. The dog knows this. Were I to begin shooting coots, he would become as alert to their movements as he is now to the movement of ducks, and would retrieve them just as eagerly. This dog will even accompany me fishing and become excited when I hook a trout.

It is not the prey that excites the animal, but the act of seeking prey, and if the human partner of the expedition selects one prey but not another, that change of the rules is entirely acceptable to the dog.

In some mysterious way the wild creatures also know when they are and are not prey. On opening morning last year I paddled to within ten feet of a big coyote who watched us approach with a friendly interest quite devoid of fear. There is some recognition, not clearly definable but known to all who hunt, between hunter and prey. It gives rise to a common tradition among so-called primitive people that it is not the hunter who seeks the prey but the prey who seeks the hunter.

When it is light enough and legal enough I shall begin shooting, and at this moment of writing I have no idea whether I shall be dropping birds into the marsh or not. That is the way it is with shotgun shooting.

You shoot a rifle with the logical side of the brain, calculating distance, wind, and the pulse of your heart. But the other side of the brain fires the shotgun. The rising bird, the lift of the gun to the shoulder, the swing of it, and the motion of the boat—none of these are individually calculated. The situation is grasped in its entirety, perhaps correctly, perhaps not, but certainly intuitively. When the gun is back at your side and the bird tumbling out of the sky, you still do not know precisely how you shot or where.

When the shotgun shooter is at ease with himself, with his companions, with his world, then he will hit; when not, he will not.

True, there are men who always hit their bird. It must be a terrible thing to have happen to you, the sport of it all being removed from it as by a surgeon's quick, cold knife. Whom the gods detest they first make perfect.

On Monday, I shall hit some and miss some. Chilco will go off the canoe's bow like a rocket, hit the swamp swimming, and crash into the tall and tawny high grass above the creek, half swimming, half wading in mud. His head will switch back and forth as he takes wind scent on a downed bird. He will be lost to sight much of the time and traceable only by the sound of him thrashing through that difficult cover. When there is stillness, you know that he has found the bird and is picking it up and will soon be coming over the side of the boat with it, carrying his pride like an army with banners.

When the shadows grow long in the afternoon he and I will go back to camp, tired, dirty, and joyous beyond all measure. We probably will not have a limit of birds. Our marsh isn't that good a hunting area. But because it is not great, we shall doubtless have had it all that day for our own, no other human in sight or sound.

We shall have watched the sandhill cranes, the first birds to migrate out of the high country, as they circled high above us making their odd, old-maid titters. Tiny green-winged teal will have come over us making noises like jet aircraft by the set of their wing feathers. On the horizon, past the golden leaves of poplars and the deep green of pines, we shall have seen the snow of the high mountains forty miles distant, shining in the sun. With luck and hard work, we will have lost no birds that were hit.

People say, why is it necessary to kill the birds? Why isn't it the same thing to prove your skill at shooting by firing at clay pigeon targets, why isn't it the same test of hunting to photograph the ducks?

The answer is that it is not the same, that's all. My dog understands that and so do I.

Robin Hood
Packs a Bucket of Piss

|||

BIG CREEK—One of the reasons that Robin Hood keeps getting such a good press is that he used the bow and arrow. The bow is a simpler, a finer, a more manly weapon for killing deer and tax collectors than the rifle.

British Columbia hunters have noticed this, and in recent years in which bow hunting licences were recorded separately from gun licences between 2,000 and 3,000 of them hunted Robin-Hood-style.

To others who crave the fine simplicity of it all, there are just one or two things to be pointed out.

For one, the bow Robin Hood used is out of style. The English longbow was made of yew and in a cold, damp climate it was the ideal instrument for flinging arrows about. However, during the Crusades it was found that in hot, dry regions, like the Middle East or Hell, the Turkish recurve bow outshot the yew.

But that was a minor change. It was in this century that the whole sport was revolutionized by plastics, laminating glues, and computers that calculate the aerodynamics of it all. What happened, in short, was that the Americans got hold of bows and arrows and, in their usual way, set about remaking, improving, updating, and remodelling.

That's the American way. The first white Americans came to this continent, found a place with lots of fishing and hunting, no taxes, and women who did all the work—and they insisted they could improve it.

They improved the bow into what is called the Compound. It is built of plastics, rare Brazilian hardwoods, glass, and steel, it has cables and pulleys, and it resembles Lions Gate Bridge.

There is, as you might expect, an improvement on the Compound, a cam pulley that adds not less than 12 or more than 20 per cent in ballistic force.

Arrows are made of aluminum and the bird feathers at the end have had to go. The rustle that feathers make is aerodynamic loss, plastic imitation feathers add .73 per cent to release velocity, and who does not want more release velocity?

Don't take my word for it. Read any archery magazine.

There are snap-on plastic arrow nocks that hold firmly and release cleanly, a stabilizer that mounts on the bow to lessen torque. There are, as God is my witness, telescopic sights for bows. Another type of sight has a battery light that makes the sight easily visible in early dawn or late dusk, should you wish to shoot apples off your kids' heads before breakfast or after supper.

There are range finders and there are devices for setting the arrow in firing position and carrying it that way, half-nocked, you might say. There are arrows with hoops in front for shooting birds on the wing and arrows with line and harpoon heads for shooting fish.

You can buy something called a Spinsert (no, stupid, Maid Marian was a spin*ster*) and this will cause your arrow to spin while in flight, "increasing penetration by eliminating loss of energy caused by side torque."

The Pore Ol' Tom Company of New Jersey manufactures a Sidewinder arrow that is stainless, ball-bearinged, grooved, has a one-piece bumper pin, and goes fifteen feet per second faster.

Changes to hunters are more vivid and arresting.

They dress in camouflage suits and wipe nonallergenic paint on their faces. Obsessed, as Americans ever have been, by the subject of body odour, they chew special chlorophyll tablets and douse themselves with Essence of Skunk or Essence of Fox on hunting day morning so they will be mistaken for somebody else. (The essence manufacturers, devoted as usual to research, report that to mask human underarm odour requires more Essence of Fox than Essence of Skunk. Remember that.)

Archery hunters hang from trees on patented platforms, waiting for deer to pass beneath them. There are more devices for getting hunters up into the trees than B.C. high riggers ever learned. Spikes, pulleys, nylon cable, safety belts, and a bucket of female deer urine which you hoist up after yourself and drip to the ground so that buck deer will come your way.

In Texas, where the thinking is big, one company has done better. Noticing that Nature is notoriously careless in her placement of trees, this manufacturer produces a prefabricated tree of aluminum poles, painted in camouflage of course. It weighs only fifty-five pounds and can be assembled where a tree should have been, if only Nature were more orderly.

So, on the opening day of deer season, the modern Robin Hood is dressed in camouflage suit, grease paint, and de-scented boots; he smells of Fox Essence, Skunk Essence, and, for good measure, some Pine Scent, Earth Scent, and Corn Scent.

In one hand he carries a Compound bow with cam pulleys, six kinds of arrows, finger guards, wrist guards, stabilizers, scope sight, range finder, and wind detector.

Moving left across his bellybutton, which is hidden by his no-glare deer hunter's belt buckle, he carries in his other hand deer calls, aluminum-plated survival blanket, maps, compasses, and his fifty-five-pound prefab aluminum portable tree. In this hand he also packs a bucket of doe piss.

It may not be exactly what Robin Hood or the back-to-nature people had in mind.

Beef

|||

To the best of my knowledge and belief, when weaned I went straight from my mother's breast to a beef standing rib roast. I was well along in years, old enough to view girls as sexual objects, before I learned that there were meats other than beef. Pork and chicken, for instance. That is if you can call chicken meat.

When a Newfoundlander speaks of having fish, he means codfish and no other type of fish. When a Nova Scotian takes a drink, it is rum. Other beverages are called what they are: whiskey, gin, and brandy. But when a Bluenoser says drink, he means rum. In our family the word meat meant beef.

I have eaten beef in every form: the roasts, preferably bone-in, the steaks by threescore and ten different names, stew meat, ground meat, tongue, tripe, liver, kidneys, and prairie oysters.

I have eaten it fried, boiled, baked, and barbecued. I have gulped it raw and I have gnawed it as jerky, roasted it on long sticks, and baked it underground.

In the Chilcotin I have eaten and invariably enjoyed the nameless, haphazard cuts they make on a loin to get that regional dish which is called Fried Meat. And it was no surprise to me when, down in Texas, I learned which beans to use in making chili con carne. No beans, that's which beans. The one true and original Texas recipe is beef and chilies with no adulterants.

Surprising it may seem, but in those many years of eating beef

I never encountered bad beef. Some beef was a lot better than other beef, but there was no bad beef. No doubt that is one reason for this meat's popularity.

Of late it has befallen me to diet and I have been choking down the white meat of chicken, which puts a lump in my throat and a kink in my backbone. There is beef on my diet, but the book insists you measure out your portions by the ounce. When a man is driven to taking his beef by the ounce instead of the pound he might as well cut it out completely. A three-ounce portion is just kissing your sister.

However, this monkish abstinence from real food has provided time for reflection and just possibly some rearrangement of old ideas.

Like a few other beefeaters, including the entire population of England, I believed that overcooking was the ruination of good beef. All beef should be rare, or, better, blue. "Just polish the horns, wipe its bum, and lead it in."

Now, was this truth, or just trendiness?

If true, the tastiest beef should be eaten raw from the steaming carcass, wolf-style, and that just isn't so for those of us who are not wolves. Tartar beef is proof. Made of raw ground beef, raw egg, capers, and raw onions, tartar beef tastes of capers and raw onions, nothing more. If you add garlic it will taste of capers, raw onions, and garlic.

Truth to tell, cooking adds to the flavour of beef, and overcooking is all in your head. Out of long habit I may live out my life eating beef red, but I repent my snobbery on the subject. The way things have been in this house lately, I have had time to dig out some clear memories of having poked my knees under tables where beef was served cooked black as a banker's heart and I remember that the juices ran rich from it and the flavour was fine, yea, even splendid.

Are there other superstitions to shed?

The nearer the bone the sweeter the meat? Was this, too, just early yuppie talk?

Possibly. It has always seemed, it still seems, that the best roasts and the best steaks have a bone in them. But I shall not be adamant about this ever again, when I am permitted once more to chew domestic cow. After all, the cooks from Canton teach us that the boneless flank steak, the least regarded of all the steaks in Anglo-Saxon cookery, can be one of the finest.

As to fat. Ah, fat. One weeps. Fat is to beef what cheese, port wine, and cigars are to a banquet. All the fats are different. Some bubble, some are marbled, some snap and crackle, and each has its particular and unique flavour.

But it is time to confess that the exterior fat of a beef is good only once, when it comes hot from the oven. When cold, it doesn't taste all that much better than tallow candles. Not everything in our world is perfect, not even the fat on beef.

It is true that supermarket beef is inferior to what our fathers knew. In earlier and happier times, steers were old enough to have ribs the size of telegraph poles when they went to slaughter. They were big, mature animals and, on a varied diet of natural wild grasses, they acquired flavours such as cannot be found in the near-veal we are taught to buy.

The fat of these old, grass-fed animals was yellow, like good butter, and rich, like the meat itself. It wasn't necessarily tender. You couldn't cut it with a fork. But people who want food that cuts with a fork should stay with oatmeal porridge.

Yet, though my soul pants for old beef, I will condemn no beef merely because it is young and tender. In the contrite spirit that comes from feeding on chicken and grapefruit, I would welcome a cut of slinky Calgary grain-fed, should no robust stuff be available, and I would refrain from invidious comparisons.

Also, I have learned to wait.

Somewhere down life's long trail I know there waits for me a six-year-old dry cow who went poor over a hard winter and then gained rapidly in spring and early summer on wild grasses, a cow that went to her death fat and happy, as we all should hope to do someday. And from her will be removed a standing rib roast that we shall cook with no fancy sauces, because the better the meat, the less important the cookery. There will be no damn grapefruit served at that meal either.

I think of that animal often.

Old Friends, Old Dogs, Old Roads, Old Whiskey

|||

QUILCHENA—Memories are odd things. Odd when they fail and odd when they work.

So it is this September morning, driving the thirteen or fourteen kilometres of old Merritt-Kamloops highway that wind beside lovely Nicola Lake.

Started driving it a bit past the ranch of the late Colonel Goldman (noted for his skill in playing the zither) as cross as two sticks because lack of memory left my denim jacket hanging in the clothes closet. Up in the interior country for weeks of travel and I forgot the one item of clothing I use the most.

Can it be that I am getting to the age when you can tell the name of every kid that came to your fifth birthday party but you don't know where you put the car keys?

Then it is Nicola Lake in the September morn, and memories crowd in, leap, dance, and sing in the clear air. Memories so great that some of them aren't even mine, they are borrowed and only seem to be part of my life.

The Maclean boys came through here after their futile attempt to start an Indian revolt in B.C. and the youngest of them, the one who killed the policeman, went to the gallows at age fifteen, the youngest person ever executed in Canada. There is a picture of this child, manacled hand and foot, taken in the B.C. Penitentiary compound.

Near the eastern end of Nicola Lake is the Douglas Lake Ranch, not the biggest but probably the best big one in B.C. Next door to Douglas Lake is where the first Guichon settled, begetting Guichons to carry the name all over the province. He was from Savoy where the people are never certain, century by century, whether they are French or Italian.

My own memories of all I ever learned about B.C. ranching began near the Nicola Lake when I set out, on a late spring night, to find the cow camp of cowboys driving out to summer range. I drove an Austin 40 station wagon then and it looked like the vehicle used by the district's Watkins salesman. I will never forget the disappointment of the oldest cowboy in camp when he learned that I was nothing but a travelling newspaperman and had no Sloan's Liniment.

There is another memory of a summer day, driving the Nicola Lake twists after running my dog in a field trial at Courtenay Lake on the Princeton-Merritt road. I was headed for Glimpse Lake, and fishing. But I had driven most of the previous night after working all the day before at the *Sun,* which pressed the reporters' noses far closer to the grindstone then. I was exhausted. I fell asleep, and I woke up to feel the car slamming against the right-hand cutbank.

The car (another A40) wasn't much damaged but I was so frightened that I am not sure I ever told anybody about this until today.

Nobody knew I was headed for Glimpse, so it's funny how things happen. If I had gone asleep on a left-hand corner instead of a right-hand corner I would probably still be in Nicola Lake, and my dog, who did not deserve such a death, would be there too, because all the windows were closed.

There's the memory of another dog on this piece of road. Rosco was his name. On a fall day I shot a duck in a slough beside Nicola Lake and, this being before I had dogs of my own, I went to the Guichon Ranch and borrowed Rosco to retrieve it. He was a Chesapeake about the size of a Shetland pony.

I took Rosco to the scene of the killing and sent him for the dead bird. He started well and because at that time I didn't kill many birds I shot at, I became very excited and shouted encouragement to him.

"Atta boy, Rosco, atta boy," I kept saying. I should have remembered that the Guichons speak no more than is necessary.

Maybe a dozen or so words a day. Rosco had never heard so many words. He turned a couple of times, trying to shush me, but when he couldn't he came back to my side, covered with lily pads but without the duck. He could not tolerate all that chat.

So I drive into Laurie Guichon's, Laurie being a fourth-generation rancher in the area, and look up his old man, Gerard.

The old road I have driven around Nicola will be half forgotten soon, says Gerard. The extension of the Coquihalla Highway into Princeton is being built far north of Nicola Lake. This will be a side road and not many travellers will see it any more.

Gerard finds a bottle of whiskey that needs demolition. Three-quarters of it is goddamn government taxes and most of what is left is water, but it is still good, like old friends, old roads, and old memories.

Never Take a Job

|||

PENDER HARBOUR—An appealing characteristic of Sam Lamont is that he used to break into prison.

Most people want to break out of prison. Bill Miner did it from the B.C. Penitentiary in New Westminster and set a kind of pattern for that sort of thing in this province. But Sam Lamont is a man who can always sense the popular trend and turn against it, like a spawning salmon. He broke into prison and stole, which rates a separate section of the Criminal Code.

The break-ins occurred while he was a kid, living near Burnaby Lake, during the late twenties. Oakalla Prison Farm had bought piles of lumber, with which the authorities intended to rehabilitate the King's guests with some sort of uplifting self-help projects. Sam and his pals wanted to build rafts to paddle on the lake and there was no better source of materials. By night they got over Oakalla's fence and helped themselves to two-by-fours, four-by-eights, and plenty of tongue-and-groove, all Grade A cedar.

Their rafts, some of the most expensive ever built by small boys in this province, introduced Sam to the idea of travel by water. He never learned anything else. Now, when he has passed the age when Her Majesty gives the golden handshake, he still does not know how to drive a car.

Car drivers are among those things in life that he finds to be unlovely. His handsome home on a point of land at the edge of Garden Bay is the last house on the road.

"We put up a sign saying Private Road. The car drivers all come down to see how private it is. Then we tried a sign saying Dead End Road. Now they drive down to see how dead it is."

Beside the house is his private dock, set on a narrow neck of the salt chuck, and tied up at his private dock is his private live-aboard sailboat. He has power machinery enough in the basement of the house to equip a profitable cabinetmaking factory and, from the windows upstairs, a million-dollar view.

In the kitchen, Ann, his companion of many years, is apt to be baking pastry and cookies on any given day. "Don't congratulate her on the cookies," Sam will say. "She cooks such a godless quantity of biscuits and stuff that one or two things are bound to turn out right, even if only by accident."

Ann ignores that. She often ignores him. It may be that, like a few other men, he repeats himself from time to time and laughs at his own jokes.

Sam and Ann are a vivid contrast. He is built one man high and two men wide, roars instead of using a speaking voice, and has untrimmed eyebrows, bushy as pine boughs, that poke out over shining blue eyes.

Ann, who was a nurse, is a Brit—neat, trim, and with some of the strength and brittleness of good English bone china. Whenever she and Sam are introduced she insists on introducing herself. After Sam says, "I'm Sam Lamont," she instantly adds, "And I am Ann Clemence." Ann is a feminist of the blue-rinse school.

For more years than he cares to remember Sam was a licensed beachcomber. He would have been happier working as an unlicensed beachcomber but a man has to surrender to government once or twice in a lifetime. He sold his beachcombing tug, which was strong and wide, like him, a few years ago. He and Ann spend much of their summers cruising the B.C. coast in their sailboat, roaming as far north as Alaska.

Sometimes they pick up some extra money by caretaking a logging camp during a winter shutdown. Except for a few tasks like driving a car or attending tea parties, Sam seems the man who can do anything, find anything, make anything.

Asked some years ago to keep an eye open for a chunk of pencil cedar big enough to make a mantelpiece, he and Ann turned up at the house with an eight-foot, two-inch-thick plank on the roof of her Volvo. He had chainsawed it out of some unbelievably big log. Most people don't know pencil cedar can grow so big.

No charge, he said. "Some day you'll get a flat tire at our house and I'll charge you a hundred bucks for the loan of my jack. Everything evens out in time."

Roaring and snorting like an old sea lion on its rock at the harbour mouth, he continues to exert a powerful attraction for many friends and to draw at least the curiosity of strangers. He claims to have no use for babies, although he fathered some in a previous marriage and is now a grandfather. "Woman wants to show me her baby I say the hell with it, ma'am. Like oranges, babies all look the same."

In such fashion his life proceeds about as free from bile and blisters as any inhabitant of this land you might easily find.

When asked why a teetotaller who is built like a rum puncheon should have such good luck in this world, Sam offers a simple formula, the one he followed all his working life: "Never, ever, take a job. It will prevent you from doing anything in this life."

The advice comes late for some of us who went to sixty and more before quitting. But then, if we had torn ourselves free of the wage economy forty years earlier, we might have ended up like Sam Lamont, a character. Who would want that?

A Writer's Handbook
|||

Those of us who make a sort of living from writing books are often asked to explain how it is done.

Any author, when asked, will answer. Authors feel a public duty to guide people. It doesn't matter to where, as long as it's guidance. Politics is the same.

A standard question is: *How long did it take you to write your latest book?*

You may reply: "All my life, up to that point." This sounds impressive enough but some people out there are pretty dumb and don't get the point. Others do see the point and make rude remarks. A writer who hasn't won a Governor General's Award or received a Canada Council grant shouldn't fool around with answers like that.

A better rule for authors asked the "how long" question is to take the date on which the thought of writing the book first strayed in behind their eyebrows. Next, include the couple of years when you forgot you even had such an idea. Add in all the holiday time, diverted time, falling-down-drunk time, and time the manuscript spent in the mails going from publisher to publisher; also the hours spent in fishing when thinking about maybe getting at that damn book for real.

Take all this time, multiply by 7, divide by 2.7, and you will have a fairly impressive figure. If you don't have a digital calculator, divide by 2.

No writer sane enough to be allowed outdoors without a keeper

ever answers the question honestly, whether it refers to the time
it takes to write a book, a play, a TV script, or shorter-time items,
such as newspaper columns. There are fees involved, you know.

Where do you get your ideas? is another popular question.

From other writers, of course. Did you think we got them out of
Chinese fortune cookies?

There are a very limited number of stories in this world and
writers keep telling them over and over again. Even in the cold
world of fact, into which newspapers occasionally stray, the number of stories is small. Heroic Coughing Dog Warns Family of
Fire still gets retold once a month. Only the place, date, and
names alter.

All the good stories got told some time before *Homo sapiens*
learned to write, so the slender stock of stories has to be traded
around. If you like the word stolen, use it.

This may make writers seem unoriginal. They are. But note
that Shakespeare, a popular although semi-literate Brit who
sometimes spelled his own name wrong, continues to get a good
press although he is dead and divested of all royalty rights. Nobody mentions that he stole half his stories from Plutarch's *Lives*
and the other half from *Burke's Peerage*.

I have written a book. What do I do to find a publisher?

Pour gasoline over yourself and strike a match on your fly zip-
per at halftime in the Grey Cup game. Being a celebrity is more
important than knowing how to spell.

*Is it important to spell correctly or to construct complete
sentences containing nouns and verbs in proper sequences?*

A significant body of opinion in the writing community holds
that knowledge of grammar is not necessary and may be harm-
ful. It is felt that important matters are Concern, Involvement,
and Ecology. Publishers are resisting this trend but perhaps only
because publishers have a lamentable tendency toward mer-
cantilism.

*I have a slender volume of verse ready for a publisher but be-
fore I let one of them see it, how do I protect myself against
plagiarism?*

This is a hard one and it is best met openly, frankly, and
directly.

Sir or Madam, your verses are not going to be stolen for the same reason that K Mart's Timex watch counter is safe from the depredations of the Great Train Robbery gang. Instead of worrying about theft, why don't you walk down to English Bay beach, bring your hand back well behind your head, and pitch your slender volume of *pensées* as far as they will go into the chuck?

Let's you and me make a lot of money. See, there's this diary my uncle wrote about his ten years as stableboy at the racetrack. He didn't write it at the time, he wrote it twenty years later, but boy is it ever interesting . . .

No.

Let's you and me make a lot of money. See, I've got the idea, and you know how to write it down . . .

No.

Are you working on a new book?

Answers, to be used at random, are yes, no, and well, one is in the preparation stages. Most find it helpful to give answers by fixed days, Mondays for no, Tuesdays for yes, and so on. Any time you are confused, as in leap years, start with yes.

Is one time better than another for writing?

Certainly, yes, just as one time is better than another for cleaning out the septic tank.

I simply don't know how you people do it.

What gave you the impression that we knew?

The Saskabush Galápagos

| | |

About the only reason for a tourist to turn off the Trans-Canada Highway and drive into Piapot, Sask., is a suspicion that he's getting a flat tire.

It will do him no good. There is no garage in Piapot. Like almost all other town enterprises, it withered and died years ago in the dust storms, the heat, the cold, the all-round hellishness of the economy on the bald prairie.

Apart from a lot of boarded-up houses there isn't much left of Piapot. One of the three original grain elevators remains. There is a provincial works department garage where the white-tailed deer come to the irrigated lawn to feed at evening. There is one hotel with scrolled-tin ceilings; twelve rooms, one bathroom, rate ten dollars a night. It has a beer parlour stuffed to busting by one old pool table and two patrons who have been declared historic sites by the Saskatchewan Heritage Branch.

Piapot is, then, a stereotype of a dull, dying old Saskabush town and I count myself lucky that I wheeled the riceburner in there a while ago because I was taught, yet one more time, to never, never, never believe in stereotypes. Only Hollywood movie producers become famous and successful by believing in stereotypes.

The first indication that things are not exactly as they seem came when it turned out that the hotel serves meals by appointment only—long in advance, please. And it's not pork chop with peasencarts, it's pheasant under glass, quail, bouillabaisse, and the like.

The customers came from Maple Creek, half an hour's drive west, and Swift Current, an hour to the east. Also California, if only because there is no place in North America untouched by a California licence plate.

The owners were Dick and Hazel Murdyk. He started as a pipeliner and she as a schoolteacher. (If you're interested, St. Paul was a soldier before he walked the road to Damascus. Nobody can predict where we will end up.) The Murdyks turned out to be people with interests seven leagues beyond glazed salmon and quiches. Witty, well read, and with so many interests and hobbies that every day in Piapot was ended before they were.

Using metal detectors, they hunted CPR construction camps of the last century. The biggest camp, nearest to Piapot, eluded them, although there had been a thousand men shedding old coins and Prince Albert Tobacco cans there. They know local history and can expatiate on the old 76 Ranch, which reached from Piapot to the American border and was a bigger unit than can be found anywhere outside Australia, Mongolia, and possibly—once you remove the bull and buckshank—Texas.

The Murdyks can tell you where the antelope play in Palliser's Triangle. Like some humans, antelope are direly afflicted with curiosity. If you tie a piece of toilet paper to your car aerial and play the radio loudly, sooner or later antelope will walk over to see just what on earth it's all about, and you may then photograph them or shoot them, according to your tastes and the care and attention of Her Majesty's game wardens.

With such an introduction to what I had thought to be an inconsequential pimple on the bare ass of Canada, I used up three days in the Cypress Hills, Maple Creek, and the region generally.

That was only enough to learn that in a dreadful year of drought, Skull Creek has a bumper wheat crop; and that the Cypress Hills are a sort of dryland Galápagos with wild turkey, horned toads, moose, elk, a lake, golf courses, hotels with bathrooms in all the rooms, and rare species of plants.

Also that there are fifty-foot sand hills, walking across the land at the rate of ten feet a year yet, within two hoots and a holler of a delightful regional camping park with a lake, trees, a small golf course and torrents of wild birds.

As the meanest intellect eventually grasps, on the Prairies there is no single weather pattern, social pattern, or any other pattern. It isn't true, what we say about the sameness of that land. It rolls, folds, dips, and unfolds; it is by turn desert, the sown, and the land of Eden without the apple, but also without the snake.

Apart from golden cathedrals with beggars on the front steps— a European specialty—there isn't much a tourist can't find in the Saskatchewan dust bowl. Anyway, I prefer antelope to cathedrals. If you have seen one Sistine Chapel you have seen them all.

So I am grateful to Piapot, even though the Murdyks left a while ago and set up their gourmet restaurant in Shaunavon, where there are more than seventy-five people left.

Corporate Welfare Bums

|||

You and I, friends, are about to bail out another big industry. This time, unless some unusually diligent free-enterpriser gets his snout into the public trough first, we are going to bail out the oil industry.

The Alberta government is already doing it. Ottawa won't be far behind.

We don't yet know how the federal government will elect to hand out welfare money to the oil people, those ardent opponents of government interference in the marketplace. It probably won't be a direct subsidy. It will probably be in the form of tax forgiveness.

Tax forgiveness means that the taxes of ordinary people are kept high so that the taxes of a few lucky companies can be made low, and those who do the paying—you and I, brother and sister— may be forgiven for not showing much appreciation of the difference.

Of course for those who subscribe to the money-tree theory of public finance, it really doesn't matter. The government, being the creator of all money, can print as much as it wishes and give away all it chooses.

The number of ordinary citizens who adhere to that belief is small. Most people know that they create this nation's wealth, not the governments, and they recognize that when governments hand out tax money as welfare payments to one or another corporation there is less for the multitude of us to share.

When the people David Lewis so aptly called corporate welfare bums get our money, the route this process takes is often so indirect that the citizen can scarcely track it.

All automobile prices, for instance, are higher than is justified. This is because the Canadian auto industry, an infant some eighty years of age, still demands shelter against foreign competition while it is growing to maturity. Once a big business learns to suck, it is almost impossible to shake it off the government tit. So it obtains a season pass to the ordinary person's bank account by coaxing government to keep the competition out. A tariff is one method.

The Japanese, whose cars so many people on this continent prefer, are also limited here by what are absurdly called voluntary quotas, buzzwords that are supposed to make us believe that the Japanese don't really want to sell a lot of cars.

Such tricks and stunts enabled the Big Three domestic manufacturers to report profits in 1985. As for the Japanese, since demand for their cars exceeds supply, some of them now withhold the simple economy models from the Canadian market and fill their voluntary quota with luxury models that not everybody would prefer, had we a true free-enterprise economy with genuine competition.

Who pays the bill? You do. I do.

Now and then our auto industry goes further, as when Lee Iacocca insisted that the Canadians go good for the $200 million he wanted for executive salaries and other needs of his corporation. Chrysler has since regained financial strength (in part because American and Canadian governments agreed that the Japanese competition should have one hand tied behind its back) and Mr. Iacocca feels free to write a book demanding that government keep its hands off the free-enterprise economy.

It is even rumoured the old hypocrite may run for U.S. president. On a free enterprise ticket, of course.

In Japan, people like Iacocca would have no platform from which to lecture us on the virtues of open competition. Managers there are vulnerable. Like other governments, the Japanese sometimes consider it necessary to rescue a failing industry. However, there is a condition attached to the bailout. The managers under whom the corporation got into difficulty must all be fired before there is the layoff of a single rank-and-file worker.

Think about this if you sometimes wonder why Japanese industry leads the world.

True, free enterprise and open competition exist in Canada. I am personally acquainted with some who are involved in that process.

For instance, Peter, who, with a clutch of relations, operates a grocery store. Peter is free to compete with all the other grocers and, if he mismanages, indeed, if he merely has a run of bad luck, he is entirely free to go broke and shut his doors.

From the Atlantic to the Pacific there are tens of thousands of small businesspeople who compete and live or don't and die. But not big corporations. Governments declare them to be immortal.

The most appropriate quotation here is a variation of one popularized by Marx: From each large corporation according to its ability (assuming it has any left), to each large corporation according to what it perceives to be its needs.

Sometimes the needs would surprise little free-enterprisers like Peter.

Gulf Oil, one of the beneficiaries of the Alberta taxpayers' involuntary generosity, couldn't have been too hard up. It had enough money to go into the liquor business, buying up one of the country's largest distilleries, even as it was standing rattling its tin cup at the legislature doors.

One of the outstanding welfare bums of all time must be the great international conglomerate AT & T, which most recently distinguished itself by paying big money to get rid of a left-wing government in Chile.

During the Second World War, AT & T fought for both sides. In the United States it made guidance systems for the American bombers and in Germany it made Focke-Wulf fighters designed to shoot down the American planes.

There was nothing unusual in this. It is, in fact, inevitable that branches of a multinational company will be enlisted by the country in which they are located whenever there is a war. What made the AT & T case different is told in an excellent book called *The Screwing of the Average Man* by David Hapgood.

When history's worst war ended, when the last of the dead had been buried, AT & T went after the American government for the damage caused to its AT & T German fighter-plane factory by the AT-&-T-equipped American bombers. The United States foreign claims department gave the company $27 million of the American taxpayers' money in compensation. Some of those taxpayers had sons who died flying their country's bombers against Nazi Germany.

For mindless greed, this is perhaps matched only by the Canadian company, Falconbridge Nickel, whose president reported thusly to the shareholders during the dark, hard days of 1943:

"Understandably, you will be glad to hear, as I was, through indirect channels, [that] your Norway refinery is safe so far and is being maintained. It is in operation by your Norwegian staff under German control on the same Norwegian nickel-copper ore."

Britain, Russia and the rest of us felt we had our backs to the wall. Falconbridge's executives were cheerful about the state of the company property and didn't seem to mind in the least about their copper and nickel supporting the German war machine.

Such are the corporate welfare bums which you and I support, like it or not, know it or not, with our taxes.

There are times I think I would rather spend my tax dollars buying whiskey or hunting dogs or even giving a bit more help to widows and orphans. But that is not to be.

The More the Laws,
the More the Criminals

|||

Almost all of 1984 lurched past without me being reminded, with undue savagery, of what George Orwell wrote about the year. It seemed we might make it to 1985 with no more than the usual awareness of Big Brother.

We didn't quite. On December 22, Toronto's *Globe and Mail* spoiled it all by reminding us that Newspeak and all the other horrors Orwell foresaw are with us in the here and now, and have become socially acceptable.

In the *Globe and Mail*'s column called "The Ottawa Scene" appeared these lines: "A crude measure of the efficiency of a legislature is the number of government bills passed per sitting day."

There it is, the naked truth of our age. The worth of a government is to be measured by the speed with which it can wrap chains around the citizenry.

The *Globe*'s columnist then reveals to us the best and the worst governments of Canada.

Among the provinces, it seems that Quebec's legislature is the least vigorous in harrying the people who elected it. That legislature averages only forty-three government bills passed into law for every 100 days it sits.

British Columbia was almost as bad. Our legislature put through only forty-seven for every 100 sitting days.

The most efficient ("most efficient" are the *Globe*'s words) were New Brunswick's legislators. The ardent democrats of

Fredericton think up and enshrine in statute 138 pieces of legislation for every 100 days they sit.

New Brunswick, you will see, put new restrictions upon New Brunswickers at the rate of one and a third per day. They must have a shorter lunch hour in the legislative restaurant.

Next, the *Globe* reports upon the national government, which is in simply terrible shape. In 100 sitting days, the federal Parliament usually passes only twenty-one government bills.

True, the Ottawa Parliament sits longer than do provincial legislatures. A bill passed every five days still adds up to scores more laws per year. Think of this going on year after year, as it has, and you get a pretty decent addition to the 40,000 or so laws and regulations punishable by imprisonment which our great democracy has produced to date.

But to the *Globe*'s columnist, Ottawa's record is pretty shabby: "If lawmakers are elected to make laws, those who get sent to Ottawa appear to do the poorest job of any legislature in Canada."

In the great parliament of Locri every representative who stood in the house to urge passage of a new law or regulation to restrict his fellow citizens wore a rope around his neck. The rope was removed only after the parliament approved the new law. If the parliament did not approve, the rope was used to strangle the gentleman.

This sort of reverence for freedom would astound and dismay the *Globe*'s columnist and a hundred, a thousand other newspaper people in 1984. They have been raised to believe that the purpose of government is to legislate people into Heaven.

I served in the twenty-eighth Parliament of this country and in those four years we approved, I am sure, our sad quota of a couple of thousand new laws and regulations.

In that time, we found only one law to abolish. It was the witchcraft law. Thanks to the twenty-eighth Parliament, you are now free to ride over town on a broomstick if you choose, provided of course you follow Transport Canada regulations.

But that was all. At a rough calculation, the number of laws and restrictions passed outnumbered the number from which Canadians were freed by more than 100 to 1.

Some people have noticed, in recent decades, that the Niagara of legislation has not washed the tears from the face of human-kind. Somehow, sadness persists.

But any addict can explain that. We didn't pass enough laws to make the great plan work. Just a few more and things will be dandy. Perhaps a mere 10,000 or 20,000 more laws are all that is needed. Then there will be no more unkindness among us, nei-ther will ringworm nor tooth decay be permitted, and never again will it rain on a national holiday.

It's a pity it takes so many police officers and jails to make the system work. ("The more the laws, the more the offenders," was the proverb quoted in the Law Reform Commission of Canada re-port of 1976, when we ran 10,000 or so short of the number of laws we have today.)

It's also a pity that there are practically no societies in today's world, and not one in history, where citizens needed as many lawyers to explain their rights to them as do the Canadians today.

Never mind. Big Brother says laws are all for our own good. So does the *Globe and Mail*.

George Orwell didn't say so, but he is dead, and doesn't matter.

Land and Liberty,
Canadian-style

|||

While the Lord State Almighty was still young, Canada was a much freer country than it is today. Life may not have been as fair. There was more exploitation of the poor. But freedom we knew.

Most of the things a man wanted to do—build a house, drive a car, keep dogs—he just went ahead and did. The principle was that a Canadian could do any damn thing unless there was a specific law passed to prevent him. Legislators, a generation or two ago, were reluctant law-passers.

Now we have created the State Almighty. We still have the poor. We don't have the freedom. And the jury is still out on the question of whether society is fairer or not.

Consider the case of Eddy Anis Haymour v. the Lord State Almighty.

In 1971, Mr. Haymour, a Lebanese immigrant, bought Rattlesnake Island in Okanagan Lake and set about making it an amusement park with an Arabian theme.

Had you or I lived near Rattlesnake Island we might not have welcomed this development. Ice-cream parlours built in the shape of camels are not to everybody's taste. But we deal here not with aesthetics but with freedom, and how much of it a small man can snatch from the Lord State Almighty.

Having consulted a lawyer, Mr. Haymour learned that there were, at that time, no zoning or building restrictions applicable to Rattlesnake Island. Regional districts and regional zoning laws were being developed in B.C. then but there, in Premier W. A. C. Bennett's own riding, no bylaws were yet in place. They would come but, by the time they did, if Mr. Haymour had done sufficient development, he would have the right to continue his camel ice-cream parlour as a nonconforming user of the land.

It would all be legal. It would all be a legitimate exercise of freedom by one Canadian citizen.

The state, the Lord All-Powerful, brushed all such considerations aside and set about preventing the development.

This was done sometimes by bureaucrats attempting to bluff the developer, sometimes by their threatening him, and usually by their deceiving him.

By 1974, Mr. Haymour had run out of money and hope. He sold Rattlesnake Island to the government for $40,000. He had, by this time, been arrested for possession of letter bombs. He was found not guilty by reason of insanity. He spent some time in Riverview Mental Hospital. Later, in Lebanon, he became involved in a hostage-taking incident at the Canadian embassy.

Indeed, Mr. Haymour has caused a lot of annoyance, and worse, to other people, but we deal, remember, with the question of whether he is free to do what is lawful in this country.

In 1986, Mr. Haymour sued the province of B.C., which we shall, for convenience, continue to refer to as Lord State Almighty. Mr. Justice A. G. MacKinnon's judgement will chill a few hearts: "I am satisfied senior officials of government, including ministers of the Crown with the knowledge of the office of the premier, contrived to improperly curb Haymour's development.

"The [government of B.C.] had legitimate means to effectively deal with the plaintiff and stop the development. It could have expropriated lands and paid fair compensation. . . ."

What it could not do was pass regulations in bad faith, discriminate against the plaintiff, refuse to consider applications for permits on their merits, mislead the plaintiff into thinking applications were being considered on their merits, drive the value of the property down through the use of regulation, and effectively drive the plaintiff to the brink of financial disaster.

"By reasonable standards of commercial morality, the whole transaction was not fair or just . . . the [government] failed to satisfy me that the transaction was fair, just, and reasonable."

Other words in the MacKinnon judgement used to describe actions by the state against its citizen are: "charade," "deceptive," "misleading," and "highly improper if not consciously cruel."

Individual citizens who have been deceptive and cruel sometimes go to jail. Private companies that abandon commercial morality sometimes are assessed heavy punitive damages by courts.

But we deal, remember, with the Lord State Almighty. The judge found that the Crown Procedure Act, under which Mr. Haymour brought his action, can result in a right being enforced but cannot redress a wrong. "Thus, the plaintiff's claim for punitive damages must be refused."

However, in pursuit of the principle of enforcing a right, the judge ordered the B.C. government to increase its payment for the lands it took from the sick man from $40,000 to $107,000. And, because "these proceedings would not have been necessary had the defendant acted properly in the first instance," he awarded costs to Mr. Haymour.

None of us should be surprised to learn that the Lord State Almighty objects to this decision and has appealed it.

There are those who will say that Mr. Haymour had no right to offend other Okanagan Lake residents with a Coney Island on their doorstep and that the Lord State is to be thanked for preventing it, no matter what the methods used. To such people, the loss of freedom doesn't matter much and, who knows, they may now be a majority in Canada.

Others will say that freedom reigns because there are judges such as Mr. MacKinnon to right wrongs. Alas, they ignore the many Haymours who are out there today not suing the government because they can't afford to, because they don't know how to, or because they fear it. The abuse of bureaucratic power to prevent British Columbians from buying and building on Crown lands is well known.

There will also be a few who say that such things do happen, but so what? What's *what* is that eventually these things will happen to us all.

The Compleat Canadian

|||

The Average Canadian is almost certainly a mythical creature like the Unicorn, the Average American, and the Sasquatch.

Some people insist there is such a thing as the Average Canadian, but most of us say if there really is one, why hasn't he ever tried to get in touch with us?

Oh well, let's look anyway. Is he in Ontario perhaps?

He should be. Ontario believes, privately, that it is Canada. Ontario began with United Empire Loyalists who came north after the revolution because they could not abide the thought of John and Mary growing up among those horrid little American children. There have since been infusions of Orangemen and other combative Irishmen, then Italians, Greeks, Finns, and everybody else who was willing to help to fill Canada.

It's a good province, even though it's rich. Let us not talk down Ontario. But Ontarians have never quite escaped the idea that they were placed on earth as an example of what high moral standards can do for you.

The Ontarian knows there are other provinces. He is sure they are trying as hard as ever they can to be like Ontario. He has no doubt that they can be taught useful trades and in time become self-supporting. He is a good man, a constructive man, this Ontarian, but he is not typically Canadian. Sorry about that.

Newfoundland?

Only half of the Newfoundlanders were willing to join Canada when invited, less than fifty years ago. The father of the present lieutenant-governor of Newfoundland pulled down the window blinds of the family house for a week as a symbol of mourning when the vote for Confederation carried. "Her face turns to Britain, her back to the Gulf. Come near at your peril, Canadian Wolf!"

You might find a Newfoundlander who was a typical Canadian, but what good would it do you? He wouldn't want to admit it for fear of what some neighbour might say.

In the Maritime provinces—Nova Scotia, New Brunswick, and Prince Edward Island—people still call the central provinces Upper Canada. Upper Canada and the Boston States, as the U.S. is known, are where they send their young people for work, praying they won't get married and settle down there. (How do you get thirty-five Nova Scotians in a Volkswagen Beetle? Tell them it's going to Toronto.) The young do well enough in alien lands, becoming college professors, bank presidents, and, like Cyrus Eaton, industrialists. But as a model of our typical Canadian, the Maritimer needs more whittling.

Quebec is a special case. Always has been. But why deal with Quebec in isolation, even if it asks? It should be lumped in with my favourite province, British Columbia.

When I broke an oath and strayed to the wrong side of the Rockies some years ago, I was able to see both Quebec and British Columbia at arm's length. They looked alike. Each a spoiled child of Confederation. "Don't tell me what you did for me yesterday, what are you doing today?"

What the feds are doing today is never enough, and until those provinces are more grown-up, never will be. The shrinks may know why. Possible reasons are that Quebec has too many memories (the provincial motto is "I Remember"), and B.C., because of the mild climate or inbreeding, gets too many loonies, some of whom it elects to public office.

Alberta? Until recently, when New Brunswick indulged in a damn fool experiment, Alberta was the only one-party state in the nation. There, it's a Liberal sweep, then Conservative, always with majorities usual to the Soviet Union and Warsaw Pact nations.

Besides totalitarianism, Albertans love Americans, Bibles,

money, and, sometimes, God. Albertans drive at only one speed, forty, while straddling the centre line.

For many years B.C. required Alberta tourists to use yellow licence plates as a warning signal to our drivers. The Yellow Peril, we called them. They are not typically Canadian.

We seem to be left with Saskatchewan and Manitoba, while forgetting all about the Yukon and the Northwest Territories.

Exactly the point.

If anywhere, the average Canadian dwells on the big nickel-plated belt buckle of the nation, amid rivers, lakes, forest, rocks, sand, and rusty wheat. Old Stubble Jumper.

He is so racially mixed that in this generation he seldom finds time to separate the strands of his ancestry: Ukrainian, English, French, Indian, Indian-French-Scottish mixes, Polish, Bessarabian, Levantine, Jewish, American, Norwegian, Jamaican, and a dozen more. People are few, towns are small. The women get everything from the East except their babies.

The weather's awful. The first colonists couldn't raise enough wheat to make their own bread. Almost everything these people have they got the hard way. It didn't sour them or quench their absurd optimism. Tomorrow Country, they call it.

Unlike the Quebeckers, they don't have good memories. If they had, maybe they'd have left. Unlike British Columbians, their lunacies are reserved for party time; if they were incurably moonstruck they'd have frozen to death on the front steps of the Royal Bank by now.

They are quiet, indomitable, neighbourly, drily humorous, and when they get drunk they want everybody to know it.

If we must have a mythic average man figure, he's there. Take a look in Moosomin, on the Saskatchewan-Manitoba border, next time you pass through. Go slow. At 100 kilometres an hour you would miss Moosomin if you sneezed.

Chadoonya?

|||

RENO, NEVADA—"Chadoonya?" said the pleasant interviewer at the television station in old San Antonio.

By this time I had been around a few corners of the English language in the Great Republic and I knew that this was a contraction of "What are you all doing here?"

I answered appropriately, but I added that sometimes it was hard to tune the ear to American English.

Yes, she agreed, it could take some accustoming. In Texas alone, she said, there are seventeen different and readily recognizable regional accents, her own being but one of them.

For instance, she said, what would I understand from her saying "Foe cotton yawn, ahyoosma sezras."

"Just say it as you would say it on air," I answered.

"For cutting yarn, I use my scissors," she said, biting off each word with her teeth the way the Yankees do it.

When we went on air, she spoke that way, the same non-accent that was used by television and radio interviewers in Montana, Washington State, Colorado, New Mexico, and California. I am reminded of it here tonight in a motel room in Nevada where the television news announcer sounds almost exactly like a television news announcer in Toronto, Buffalo, or Miami.

In the television station's cafeteria, he may have said, "Awwh, I tumped mah sweetmilk," which means he spilled milk that was not buttermilk, but on air he will squeeze all the music out of his voice.

In a couple of dozen interviews on U.S. radio and TV, I met only two people who talked on air as they talked off air. One was a man in Austin, Texas, who worked for a university FM station and had not yet attained professionalism. The other was a middle-aged man at Cheyenne, who just happened to be one of those individuals of highly independent mind: he had a mad on with the U.S. defence department because his family had not yet been able to get paid for grocery bills run up by General George Washington at their store in Valley Forge one winter.

All the rest were striving to sound like . . . well, truth to tell, to sound like Canadians.

"Everybody in our business tries to get that flat sound you get in the upper Middle West of the United States," one interviewer told me. "The locus of perfectly acceptable American English seems to be about Wisconsin."

"East or west Wisconsin?"

"The centre of Wisconsin," he said.

"Why do you want your speech to come out like water dripping on a tin dishpan?" I said, forgetting for the moment that it's the way I talk.

"Because no big station in New York is going to want to hire me if I talk with a Colorado accent."

"Do you want to be hired by a New York station?"

"God forbid. Wouldn't go there for any money. But I would surely be happy to be asked. It does something for you to feel that you might be hired to work anywhere in the country."

It does something to the language, too. It pounds it flat.

As it happens, I have a Vancouver friend who can testify to the importance of talking Wisconsinese.

Although he is now so respectable you would never recognize him, in his salad days he once strayed across the Mexican border at Tijuana in a highly inebriated state with a highly nubile American girl. He wondered about getting back through U.S. immigration, since he had no business being within the U.S. in the first place.

"Say you're an American," said the girl. "We're crossing at Tijuana by the thousands every day."

"They'll recognize my Canadian accent," he said.

"Tell them you're from Wisconsin. Up there, they talk just the same way the Canadians do."

So he said he was from Wisconsin and the U.S. immigration officer said great, so was he, which town, and on that day and every day thereafter for the rest of his life my friend was not able to remember the name of a single community located in the state of Wisconsin and there was some excitement at the Tijuana border crossing that day, but all that is another story.

Well, now Wisconsin is taking over everywhere.

You can still hear, when you are down here in the U.S., some difference of accent belonging to Canada. We are the only people except the Scots who make the world house rhyme with moose. Also we speak heavily. Better becomes bedder, we say budder instead of butter. But the differences from Wisconsinese are small and not inspirational.

I am one who grieves for what is being lost. In Canada, you will never hear the lilt of a Newfoundland accent from a TV professional. Only John Crosbie, the cabinet minister, keeps the last of that music playing on the airwaves. And in the U.S. there remains scarcely a trace of the twangs, the drawls, and the other soft, strange, or sweet sounds that gave colour and variety to the language.

Bad Legends Live as Long
as Good Ones

|||

KINGMAN, ARIZONA—Every author has at least one idea that is preposterous. John Steinbeck's was that the best restaurants are the ones truckers use.

He said it in *The Grapes of Wrath*. One of his Okies driving west to California, Land of the Nut, stopped the jalopy where the truckers stopped because there, he knew, the best food was cooked.

For some reason Steinbeck readers by the myriad accepted this as gospel truth and have ever since patronized highway restaurants called Truckers' Roost, Truck Stop, and Truckers' Coffee Fifteen Cents.

All my life . . . no, not all, I plan to go on for a while . . . all my life up until last night I had accepted this buncombe for no reason known to me except that Steinbeck had said it and I hadn't thought much about it.

Not only did I believe, I urged others to believe likewise. "Look for truck stop restaurants," I said. "Those fellows know where to eat." It usually turned out the people whom I advised already knew the rule. Does everybody read Steinbeck or did other writers begin repeating him?

Last night, for the first time, I forgot about literary elegance and considered the facts. We were eating at a truck stop. The food was, well, more or less all right. Better than food in England, not as good as a baked bean supper at the Baptist church hall.

Not the fare Mr. Steinbeck had in mind, although the truckers seemed satisfied with it.

So why is it that drivers select one restaurant at which to eat and not others?

A main consideration is that it's a restaurant that stays open twenty-four hours a day. The long, lonely nights are when much of the freight moves. Vacationers commonly get off the road and into a motel by dinnertime. Travelling salesmen may keep moving until ten or eleven, and a few until midnight or 1:00 A.M.

But at 1:00 A.M., the big rigs are just beginning to paw the pavement and snort, eager to trample down a couple of hundred miles before sunup. During those hours, most of the professional drivers pause for rest and refreshment.

Another common feature of a truck stop is that there is ample room to park the big machines. The most popular truck stop restaurants have a parking lot about the size Safeway keeps, and it is available not only to drivers who want to eat but also to those who want to shut down the diesels and climb into the overhead bunk for an hour's sleep.

Diesel and gas prices are another inducement. A popular truck stop offers special prices for large, truck-size fill ups. Most truckers are in business for themselves and are as sensible as any other businessman to saving $10 out of $150.

Some of the very big truck stops, which have signs big enough to catch the attention of passing astronauts, will have sheds the size of airplane hangars where trucks can be washed, have their oil changed, tires fixed, air conditioning adjusted.

What else attracts a trucker to a truck stop?

Other truckers attract him. He wants to be among his own kind, exchange gossip, relay messages from mutual friends, get reports on weather and radar traps.

It is worth remembering that once a roadside restaurant becomes a recognized truck stop, it is guaranteed a moderately long furlough from the bankruptcy courts to which so many restaurants make their painful way. Given enough inattention to its customers, any restaurant can lose business, truck stops included. But a truck stop restaurant has a momentum which keeps running for a considerable time after they have started putting soybean in the Salisbury steak.

So far, our list of priorities hasn't mentioned the continent's finest cooking as a requirement. Well, it isn't.

If a trucker wants to dine well, he will wait until he gets home and take his wife, or somebody else's wife, to a place where they bring you the bill on a tray. While he is working, he is remarkably like newspapermen, salesmen, and downtown office workers. He wants food that is fast, familiar, moderately priced, and reasonably free of evidence of cockroaches. He does not much care how it tastes. He hasn't time to spare for tasting things.

On the edge of a four-lane interstate is not, in any case, the place where he or anybody else should go hunting for Mr. Escoffier. The rare and fine restaurants of this continent are to be found at least a couple of miles away from the freeways. They are quiet little places on quiet little streets. There is no place beside them where a trucker can park a machine the size of a freight train.

Neither does he have the time or inclination to try. The average trucker would not drive one mile off his highway to attend the Last Supper in the company of the original guests.

I hope this lays to rest Mr. Steinbeck's worst blunder, one which has puckered the intestines of a million motorists. But I doubt that it will do any good. Bad legends live about as long as good ones.

Talking Louder Won't Help

|||

There is nothing wrong with being offensive to some people. Postal union officials and people who manage magazine subscription departments come readily to mind. Offending them might improve their characters and in any case couldn't worsen them.

Giving offence is a well-established custom; in western societies the people form teams, called political parties, so they can trade mean-spirited behaviour back and forth.

Being offensive in a foreign country is quite different. It can cost you money and inconvenience. It may even be dangerous. If your behaviour poisons a few wells, fellow citizens who follow your route later will pay for it. Nobody gains, everybody loses and the pity is that all too frequently offence is given unintentionally by tourists who are, in real life, sober, decent and kindly folk who love their old mothers and contribute heavily to the Salvation Army and the whales.

There is a good Mexican example of the trouble you can make without trying. If you lift your left forearm vertically and hit the bottom of the elbow with the palm of the other hand—precisely the action you might take to swat a mosquito—you can deliver one of the more deadly of all insults. It's doubtful that many Mexicans could explain how this gesture acquired its meaning. Possibly there is no living Mexican who knows. But of its meaning, there is no doubt: it is a way of saying "Go have sexual relations with your mother." In Guadalajara the Tapatio Hotel, alert to such matters, has a leaflet for tourists with cars, warning them that tapping out "Shave and a Haircut, Two Bits" on the car horn carries the same message and must be rated dangerous. That is thoughtful service.

In Arabia, to cross your legs in such a way that you display the sole of your foot to your host is a grievous affront. In England don't refer to anybody as a good old bastard, no matter how friendly your tone and intent; the English take the word literally.

But those are among the special cases which will occur rarely and will usually be perceived as ignorance rather than bad manners, the one being better than the other.

More pervasive harm is done subtly.

Americans, Canadians and Germans have a reputation for loud talk. Those of us whose hearing is failing may see nothing wrong with clear, resonant speech but many other nationalities perceive it as arrogant and boorish.

Before they took the cure recently in the rearrangement of international exchange rates, Americans aroused distaste when abroad by waving handfuls of dollars in the air. The filthy stuff was exactly what the natives were after, but quietly, please. Some nationalities, like the British, feel that paying money for goods or services is like some of the bodily functions which, although fundamental to good health, should be conducted in private and without comment.

So many national conventions, and only a lifetime to learn them.

When taking a taxi in parts of Arabia, it is not well to say "Take me to the airport." Instead, one suggests that a trip to the airport might be pleasant; what does the driver say to such a thought?

This driver knows you want to go to the airport and nowhere else and that he is going to earn a fare by driving you there and nowhere else. But it chafes him to receive an order, when a suggestion can serve just as well.

The logic does not matter. Always keep repeating to yourself, I am not in my own country. Say it whenever you brush your teeth, provided you brush after every meal. Also say it, three times, whenever you become irritated by habits foreign to you.

The asking of directions often leads to irritation. There are only a few countries where people give good directions. Britain is one;

the bobbies there are trained to do it without ever lifting an arm
and pointing. (It is thought that if they were to point traffic might
be halted or misdirected.)

In Japan, Latin America, the Mediterranean countries and
many other places, a tourist, when lost, must make a conscious
effort to avoid being misdirected. This is done by never signalling
the kind of answer you would like to get. Say "Could you direct
me to the post office?" but never say "The post office is straight
ahead, isn't it?" The second question invites a yes or no answer
and since it is rude to say no you will be told yes, even though you
are walking directly away from the place you want to be. This
compulsion to be polite instead of helpful encourages crankiness
in a weary traveller but bite your tongue. It is their country and
their custom, not yours. Somehow, they have got along all these
years with a prohibition on the word no.

Clothing, particularly the lack of it, is a constant cause of irritation and dismay. Some reactions in other countries are predict-
able, or should be. Where women use their dress as a hiding
place, there may be toleration for foreign women in clothes that
fit them. But that toleration seldom extends to places of worship.
And clothing taboos are no longer clear-cut. In some conservative
states such as Greece, nude beaches have been established
where the foreigners may follow their peculiar custom by looking
only at one another.

Sex, of course, rears its lovely, foolish head. Poets and other
people prone to error are wrong about the language of love being
universal. Many a woman has ended a happy day in a sad dispute
with a highly insulted local man at the hotel-room door. Not
knowing local custom, she may have been putting out the wrong
sexual signals all day.

It also occurs in reverse. Liberated women of the English-
speaking world who believe Europeans and others to be more
sophisticated than men at home sometimes find they are not.
More than one young man, a misguided guide who cannot dis-
tinguish between dalliance and alliance, has forsaken his nation's thousand years of culture and travelled with his loins
ablaze to such places as Bismarck, North Dakota, where his one
true love has spoken in this way: "Juan, what a wonderful surprise. We must grab a bite of lunch some day before you go
home."

Anybody can understand why people resent tourists with attitudes of superiority. It is not always easy to recognize how easy it is to appear condescending, particularly in third world countries where so many public services are, to put it bluntly, inferior.

On a recent visit to Yemen, a tourist official assured me that, under the new republican government, all education is free, including education at the university level, and hospital care is available to all. Yet it was painfully obvious that there are so few schools, so few schoolteachers, so few universities and hospitals that his statement was preposterous. But why say so?

I responded by saying that this seemed excellent government policy. This enabled him to dispose of the matter honourably by commenting that, of course, not all the new policies had yet been fully implemented. Amity was preserved. A decade or two ago, I didn't think as quickly as that.

As if there were not problems enough, there is the matter of how we smell. Different national diets create different body odours. The average South Korean adult eats eighteen pounds of garlic per month, a thought to ponder for Canadians who don't push that much through the digestive tract in eight years. However, there are many subtler human odours which send us messages at the subliminal level, crying out that something about the person to whom we speak is unusual and probably sinister.

In such a minefield, it seems surprising that any of us cross in one piece. We do, and for good reasons.

As we near the year 2000, tens of millions of people from a hundred different nations travel abroad, if not for fun then to work. All of us know some of the errors because we have already made them ourselves. Most people also know that tourists mean profits. That always helps. And there is not much unconscious offensiveness that won't yield to the treatment of a little more knowledge beforehand, a little less haste in acting and speaking, the genuine expressions of curiosity and joy in your new surroundings and the good old simple smile.

Finally, humans being experimenting animals, we are apt to welcome the new and the strange in our lives and, even when not new, tourists are strange.

Once in Quebec City, when I was attending a changing of the guard of the Royal Twenty-second Regiment, the scarlet-coated regimental band fell silent for one of the more heavy moments of that solemn function and a proper hush descended on us. Then there floated overhead a clear, corn-fed female voice out of Kansas: "Do they change the orchestra too?"

Was any Canadian insulted? Hardly. Bless her, she offered us that day a delightfully different perspective on a custom we had been allowing to petrify for a century or so. I remember her better than the ceremony.

Grog, Gazpacho and Gringos

|||

TEACAPAN, SINALOA, MEXICO—At 4:00 P.M. Christmas Day, the rum hot enough and the soup cold enough, it occurs to my wife Melanie and myself that not a single Mexican guest may show up for our open house.

We had invited about fifty neighbours and friends and everybody accepted. But in Mexico it is discourteous to refuse an invitation even if you haven't the slightest intention of showing up and, for that matter, may know with certainty that you will be ten kilometres up the lagoon, visiting relatives, at the time. Still, it is courteous to cheerfully accept and Teacapan, a village of fishermen and farmers, operates largely on courtesy, there being so little money around.

The courtesy of accepting an invitation you have no intention of fulfilling may not be apparent to a gringo but, then, so many things in Mexico are not.

The explanation depends upon arithmetical formula. To accept an invitation and attend is to score two points for courtesy. To accept and not attend is one positive point cancelled out by one negative, leaving you even. But to refuse the invitation and then not attend is a loss of a full two points and you are seen to be doubly ill mannered.

I hope those numbers are helpful. Things were easier to explain years ago when we spent only two or three weeks a year in Mexico. I then knew almost everything about the country and distributed cogent advice about it to people, even those who hadn't asked for any. Since we built a house here and began spending half the year in it I have come to know much less. If I am here long enough and become truly fluent in Spanish the day will arrive when I no longer know anything about Mexico and I shall have to stop writing articles like this one.

Our Christmas open house was not in the local tradition. Christmas itself scarcely is. Christmas is about the same as a Thanksgiving Day celebration in Canada or the United States. The Feast of the Virgin of Guadalupe is attended by more parades and fireworks than is Christmas and the giving of presents, until recently, was reserved for the twelfth day after Christmas at which time the Three Kings were supposed to donate. In today's Mexico, some families get gifts from the Three Kings on Twelfth Day and some from Santa Claus on Christmas Day but the gifts are small and many children get not a one.

We are serving gazpacho, a cold soup which is neither Canadian nor Mexican but Spanish in origin, and a hot buttered rum drink we call by the historic name of grog, partly as a joke, because that is an almost impossible word for a Spanish speaker to pronounce. There is beer, but no wine. This is not wine country although the people apply the word wine to every alcoholic beverage from whiskey to sherry, beer being the sole exception. For the children we have cookies and Coca-Cola, with which they may rot their white, even teeth and help maintain their nation's position as the second-biggest Coke consumer in the world.

Invitations have gone to both husbands and wives. If men come they will come alone. If women come children will automatically be included. All families divide into two parts: a man and a woman-with-children.

People may come whom we have never laid eyes upon, relatives or friends of those we invited. An invitation to one person is an invitation to anyone they choose to bring.

At 4:15 nobody has come for a 4:00 to 6:00 P.M. open house but at 4:20, so early as to verge on discourtesy by local time standards, there arrives José Ramón León Alvarado, Kacho for short. He is the village postmaster.

Rumour has it that Kacho is a Communist but he has told us that he supports PRI, the Party of the Institutionalized Revolution, Mexico's permanent governing party. He reasons that most of Mexico's problems are foreign problems and that the country needs a party experienced in foreign affairs.

In days when the Mexican peso traded higher against the U.S. dollar Kacho's salary would have been a fair one. Now a month's pay would buy him just one Cuba libre at a Mazatlán bar. He continues the service as just that, a service. It is customary to pay him the amount of postage on a letter when receiving one but even that is a puny income. He runs a little restaurant and performs other economic miracles to get along.

Many economic miracles are needed. Consider one of our local doctors who makes house calls for the equivalent of $1.20. She sells tacos in the town square each Saturday night. We call her wheeled cart The Amoeba-Free Taco Stand.

Lucilla comes with her old mother, whom we call The Grandmother. Lucilla runs one of the ten thousand corner groceries which occur in this community. We became friends when she reprimanded me once for coming into her shop and looking for what I wanted to buy. That, she said, was no way to behave in a shop. Anybody should be able to find time to pause, perhaps make a little bow, and then to talk about things which don't matter. After that one could buy a deck of cigarettes.

Next come two improbably beautiful young people, Antonio and Natalia. Antonio looks like Jesus Christ but has a better-developed sense of humour. Natalia, whose home is in the state of Nayarit, has the grace and beauty of a deer. She weeps, privately, because they have been married two years and have no children. Her husband's godfather has reprimanded her for her failure. They desperately want a baby which they will bring up, somehow, in the toolshed on the gringo's property where they help serve as caretakers.

It could be said that one more baby is one more problem in a nation where half of the population is less than fifteen years of age. But on this date we should remember that one of the world's more important people was born in a stable.

(Although we don't know it at the party, Natalia becomes pregnant at just about this date and later successfully delivers a little boy. They might have named him Grog but they didn't.)

Antonio's mother brings a present for Melanie, a purse woven of plastic cords. She is very embarrassed and apologizes that she had no paper in which to wrap the present. This puzzles us. Later we learned that the proper way to accept a present from a Mexican is to nod and put it aside to be opened after all guests have left or, perhaps, on another day. To unwrap in the presence of the donor is horridly bad manners. It is like refusing an invitation.

Antonio's mother has never had a house with a floor or windows and her life has been hard, but I have seldom known a person of such joyous animation. When Lola tells a story, and she often does, the birds stop singing so they can listen. Her face glows, her hands weave pictures in the air. Lola adorns a party.

So does Don Francisco, chemist, retired, wealthy, well read, whose wife runs a pharmacy in Tepic. Rightly or wrongly, Don Francisco is reputed to favour birth control, women's rights, Bolsheviks and just about anything else likely to be unpopular in rural Mexico, rural Mexico being like rural anywhere, bone-and-marrow conservative. Don Francisco is the Count Tolstoy of Teacapan.

Why is he accorded the title Don? Why is anybody called Don? It is perhaps easier to explain why people do *not* get the honorific title.

Nobody young is ever called Don.

Nobody is called Don merely because he is rich.

Nobody inherits the title Don.

Yet even foreigners may be called Don. One of the few Dons in Teacapan was the late Don Roberto, otherwise known as Bob Stephens, a logger from Oregon who lived his last quarter-century here without exactly the type of entry papers he needed. When the Federals came to arrest and deport him, late in his life, half of Teacapan travelled by bus and tractor to the government palace to protest and the immigration man said, "You have more friends than the president of Mexico. Go home, Don Roberto. We won't be bothering you again."

Vikina, the Widow Stephens, arrives with the daughter who was born just shortly before Bob died. The daughter is a *pocha,* a word applied to people half-gringo and half-Mexican. She has a Barbie doll. Every girl in Mexico wants a Barbie and about half of them manage to get one.

Don Francisco is dressed like his gardener but cloaked with

gentility. He ritually makes formal salutations to every person in our house. Thereafter, he tells hilarious stories about himself and other people.

His rival in anecdote is Francisco Cortez Carillo. Francisco fixes motorcycles and outboard motors and his nickname—what would you expect?—is Perumbe. It is pronounced like a forty-horse Yamaha revving: Perrooombay.

The gazpacho goes down. It was made with pepper called Tail of the Rat, which is hotter than jalapeño. Some find it too hot and set it aside but others find it bland and inspire it with squirts of Brave Sauce and Tabasco. There is no accounting for peppers.

By this time there are many children. They gravely accept cookies and candies and gravely wrap more cookies and candies in paper napkins to take home to friends. So do many adults. This has nothing to do with poverty or hunger. It is a sort of ritual sharing. Even if it isn't a feast, you share with those who couldn't come.

The síndico arrives and, like Don Francisco, makes formal rounds and executes formal gestures. At about seventy, he is the oldest man born in this place. Guadelupe Castro. Don Lupe. Known also as Toothpick because when young he was thin as well as tall. He has a foghorn voice. *Ronco,* it is called. Small boys in the village delight in inflating their chests and imitating his tone.

The mighty PRI party elects a president for a city council in the parental city of Esquinapa but in small places such as this there is no council and PRI appoints a síndico. He combines the offices of chief of police and town manager.

Don Lupe sometimes packs a revolver and often rides around town with the police in their truck. He is a man who understands waiting, keeping your own counsel and politics. He was supplanted as síndico once by a younger man but later regained office. One of the things he did was to use Teacapan's slender municipal grant to improve the graveyard. With its statues and miniature mausoleums the graveyard has now the neatest, the cleanest and the most orderly architecture of all the town. What Don Lupe remembered was a traditional saying about the Mexican, that he is in love with death and flowers.

The gringo citizenry of Teacapan need not concern Don Lupe.

They are scarce as raisins in a poorhouse bun. Doubtless we seem just as hard and dry to the local people.

What do gringos do?

Not much really.

Life here is not at all like it is in Mazatlán, which is only a little more than a hundred kilometres away. There is no tourist trade. There is not one single souvenir nor any example of native handiwork. Nobody does colourful ethnic dances.

A gringo can, if he chooses, fish the surf for corvina or run up the vast maze of the lagoon trolling for pargo and robalo. He can ride horses through the coconut and mango groves and if he loves collecting licences and permits he can get enough to shoot doves, ducks and quail in the fields. If he wishes, he is welcome to get drunk twice a day. Nobody cares.

Most of us bake ourselves on the beaches. We garden. We read a lot.

We sometimes give the appearance of having more money than brains. My favourite vignette concerns a well-to-do American, a former bomber pilot, sitting in the sun half-naked, that he might tan well, knitting a sweater—knitting being the latest of his many hobbies—and simultaneously doing guard duty on his flower plot which was menaced by iguanas. He had constructed an alarm device which involved a string tied to one big toe. He had a pistol at the ready for the first twitch of the string. He hoped to hit an iguana rather than his toe.

It is now 6:00 P.M., the hour open house ends, and the main body of guests is just arriving. People come with their own children or with others' children, with their husbands or their wives or with their alternate wives who are called Second Fronts.

Among the most decorous of our guests are a husband and wife who have not slept together for two years. She found a ten-thousand-peso bill in his pocket one night and later, after he had been absent overnight, the Mex.$10,000 was gone. It happens to be the price for one of the town's few prostitutes for one night. When he approached his wife next with heavy breathing she put out her hand and said, "The price is ten thousand pesos." The fishing has been terrible. He can't afford his own wife.

Manuel and Chevalita, who run the building supply store, arrive without their children. Typical. There is not a single stereotype of the Mexican which you cannot find utterly contradicted without stepping outside the bounds of this little community. Chevalita is a good example. She is small, dark and pretty (her name means Pretty Little One) and at first glance would serve as a model for the traditional gentle, self-effacing, obedient Mexican wife.

Chevalita does not like cooking and does not cook. She does not like housework and hires other people to do that too. She likes her children but does not dote upon them and may be one of the few mothers in the whole nation who will not spoil her son. However, she is even less interested in taking the role of paper doll. She works the hours of a typical labourer, first light to darkness. She buys and sells, orders and ships brick, stone and steel for construction projects and runs Manuel at the hard trot. The pair of them are dynamos. One of the travesties of Mexican life is the picture of the man sleeping under the cactus. Mexicans put in hours of work such as Americans and Canadians haven't known since the Hungry Thirties.

By 7:00, an hour after open house was supposed to end, the main crowd is finally present and my wife and I are tiring. Mexicans do not complain about funny words like grog or about a bathroom where there is no wastebasket in which to put used toilet paper. But a self-serve bar is beyond belief. So each of our guests must be asked over and over again if they care for more and always we must remember that the word "Thanks" means "No, thank you" except when there is a faintly different intonation in which case the meaning is "Yes, thank you."

When open house ends, a couple of hours later, the stars have come out, those big orange ones you can feel the heat from. Perumbe is winding up a hilarious story about being head-table guest at a wedding and fighting off a dog who wanted the ham bone which was wedged on his forefinger.

It's been about as much fun as you can have on a Christmas Day without snow. Simple, like the Mexican appreciation of Christmas Day; nothing more than a hot rum, beer in plastic cups and spiced soup. But a time of warmth and plain good fun. And so far as we can tell, we have poisoned no wells.

One of our few gringo guests says she admires Mexicans because they have so much fun with so little. No doubt the Mexicans wonder why gringos have so little fun with so much.

The Pistol or the Veil

|||

TEACAPAN—Sometimes I wonder if Dolores ended up in prison or a nunnery, but I will probably never know.

The village that was her home was far from here, over toward the Sierra Madre mountains that comb the eastern dawns through their saw teeth. That is a country where snow sometimes dusts the pine hills; if you half close your eyes you can believe you are at Lac la Hache in the Cariboo country.

Her name was Dolores, shortened, in the Mexican custom, first to Lola and then to Lolita. She was slender, had hair that shone, and eyes black as watermelon seeds.

She had more. There was a grace, a charm, a beauty that transcends all considerations of mere measurements. You could cover Dolores with a canvas tarp so that nothing of her showed but the tip of a little finger, and you would yet know that a beautiful woman was under the canvas.

She would not have preferred that I knew as much of her story as I did. The story came from a friend who was, like myself, practising another language. We watched that lovely young woman walk down a cobbled street and discussed idealism, youth, and the problems that arise from them.

"A quite extraordinary young woman," my friend said. "All the best of Mexican family life, and all the worst. All the best of idealism and romance, and all the worst."

Dolores was the daughter of a widower, a man who had married late in life. He had a bit of land under *ejido*, the system whereby poor Mexicans can hold and inherit the right to work lands which they do not own outright. The land of Dolores's father lay far from their little house in the village beside the mountains.

On weekends, on all the numerous school holidays, during winter and summer school breaks, Dolores arose with her father while it was yet dark and after a simple breakfast they pedalled their bicycles thirty kilometres to his fields, arriving at first light. They worked the fields until dark, then pedalled home. She then made supper and by 8:00 P.M. they slept, so they could work as hard again the next day.

"Yet he was able to keep her in high school and she was able to complete it," I said. "Quite an accomplishment."

"Yes," said my friend. "But so much work, so much that was hard, and now all at risk. Did I mention that she wants to become a nun?"

"No. Is that the risk you speak of, that a woman so feminine . . .?"

"The risk is entirely different from what a gringo Protestant could perceive."

The problem was that romance overtook the father of Dolores in his seventy-third year. He began an affair with a married woman in the next village. Neither he nor the woman was discreet.

"Dolores behaved in a quite incredible fashion. She took up the affair directly with her father. By the standards of rural, conservative Mexico, shocking.

"Not only is Dolores almost certainly a virgin, being young and unmarried it is the accepted pretence that she could not even know exactly what men and women do in bed and never should until some day she be instructed in the matter by a lawfully wedded husband. Absurdity, of course, here as in any country, but the commonly accepted absurdity."

Dolores's father was outraged, which should have silenced the girl, but she persisted, mere slip of a child though she was. She told him: "Sooner or later, one of the sons of that woman is going to shoot you."

In this, my friend noted, it could be seen that Dolores was deficient in worldly wisdom, as eighteen-year-old girls tend to be.

When a man has passed three score and ten, he knows that the time for the cashing of all cheques is not far off. If you must go, is there a better way to go than to be shot, at age seventy-two, by the son of a woman you have seduced? For a Mexican man, for many men, no.

The father said what Dolores should have expected him to say, that if God intended him to go by pistol shot fired by young men protecting their family honour, then that was God's will, and he would not stand in the way of the wishes of the Almighty.

That should have ended the conversation. But Dolores, remember, was an unusual girl. She kept talking. "Don't forget this doesn't end with you being killed," she said.

"What do you mean?" he said.

"When one of her sons kills you I will get a gun and I will kill one of them. And then I am going to spend all the rest of my life in prison and I will never get to be a nun."

"Would you do that for me?" he said.

"Yes, I would do it for you."

The father embraced Dolores and she could feel his tears on her neck.

"She tells me that now he has broken off the relationship with the married woman in the next village," my friend told me. "However, it is my personal opinion that he has only chosen to become discreet. Even when they think they are worldly, there are many things that young women do not comprehend.

"Her problem is too much youth, too much idealism, too much romanticism."

The end of this story about devotion to family, tradition, youth, romanticism, Mexico and the church is not known to me. I cannot drive back to that village to ask, because I had no right to know the beginning of the story. But I remember Dolores, the beauty of her, the way she walked, the clear light of her eyes, the clasp of that small, calloused hand.

| | |

Since writing this I have returned to that village and seen the lovely Dolores once more. She is married now and measures two axe handles across the hips but that doesn't matter, her eyes alone are enough to establish her beauty.

She illustrates a special feature of Spanish grammar. A man might say, "Dolores is beautiful," using the verb "to be" in its temporary sense. A companion, applying a different form of the verb, could properly reply: "With permission, sir, you are mistaken. Dolores is beautiful." In English the sentences "Dolores is beautiful" are identical, but in Spanish one form of the verb denotes a woman who dazzles men for the moment and the other describes a woman whose beauty is fundamental and lasts as long as she lives. The English tongue is not in all ways the most expressive of languages.

Dolores had a baby, and a husband who no doubt did not appreciate her as much as he should have. I did not inquire about her father's Second Front but I am sure that by this time she had come to terms with life's realities. Her father, I hope, appreciates an old Anglo-Saxon saying: "A son is a son till he gets him a wife, but a daughter's a daughter the rest of your life."

Cosme's Bomb

|||

TEACAPAN—The next time President Ronald Reagan takes a grand, broad view of disarmament, would he mind also taking a small, narrow view of U.S. armaments for the sake of this village?

We can't handle grand, broad armaments. We have a hard time with just one little American bomb that turned up here the other day.

I first heard about the bomb from Cosme, a boy of wide-ranging emotions, all of which display themselves vividly on his face. He rode up on his bicycle, aquiver with appreciation for death and destruction, as a healthy boy of twelve should be.

"*Bomba!* PrrrrrAOWWWW!" he cried, flinging his arms wide to demonstrate an explosion and wiggling his fingers to demonstrate the bits and pieces falling.

It took a while for us to sort this out. *Bomba* happens to be the word for water pump, of which there is about one per household, and water pumps don't ordinarily explode. It turns out *bomba* also means exactly what it sounds like.

It had not exploded, despite the fervent hopes of Cosme and all the other kids in town, but it was there just ticking away.

It had come up in shrimp nets a few kilometres out in the ocean, scooped off the sandy sea floor at a depth of about twenty metres. It was a cylinder about twenty-five centimetres in diameter and seventy-five centimetres long, badly corroded by the salt water.

On the fish-buying beach in the lagoon here, two of the fish buyers thought they recognized it as an explosive device. So they had set out to work on it with hammers and picks and managed to loosen and finally unscrew a cap. Inside was a paper.

At dark, soon after the arrival of Cosme at our house, two fishermen came with the paper to ask me to translate it. People here know my Spanish is not good, but they believe I am a heller on English. I let them believe that.

They had come to the house earlier, when only my wife was there. Since her Spanish is as good as theirs they could have asked her to translate. However, there seem to be some things, such as bombs, that are not deemed proper for consideration by women, so they waited for me to come home.

They explained that after unscrewing the first cap and finding the paper they had found a second seal with what looked like a detonating cap on the top.

By that time a considerable number of the village children had gathered on the beach, so it was thought that operations should be suspended lest Teacapan lose a part of the next generation.

My quarrel, and this village's quarrel, with the military forces of the United States is that the paper contained so much information that was useless and so little that was useful. It was, in truth, a perfect bureaucratic document—no help to anybody.

It told where the explosive had been manufactured: at an ammunition plant in Hawthorne, Nev. Also when: 1978.

It bore the signature of the inspector who found it fit to fling at America's enemies. The congressional order approving funds for its manufacture was provided, and a dozen other trivial and frivolous facts were flung in also.

Nowhere did it say whether it would explode among a bunch of Mexican youngsters. Nowhere did it say what somebody finding the device should do. Neither did it explicitly say whether it was the property of the U.S. navy or the U.S. army. For all we knew it might have been munitions some American president chose to supply to some terrorists.

With the two fishermen I drove back to the lagoon shore in their truck, a large shiny vehicle with three chrome bucking horses rearing on the hood and a pewter St. Christopher medal on the sun visor. We went to the bomb, which somebody had thoughtfully covered with a piece of nylon fishnet, much as one might, from a sense of delicacy, cover a dead body.

A goodly crowd was there.

Since the device had neither fins nor visible propulsive devices, it was not a practice torpedo or a wing rocket for planes. Probably it was a canister of explosive for insertion in naval guns. There appeared to be a detonating cap visible. We did not hammer it. People here do have some sense of caution, you know.

"What should we do with it?" said the fishermen.

I suggested they put it in the boat, sail out into the ocean and throw it back where they found it.

Failing that, I noted that the Virgin of Guadalupe celebration would come soon. Teacapan, I suggested, might have the biggest firecracker ever exploded in the Virgin's honour. That was met by loud applause. A lot of extremely funny things were said by the men, which unfortunately went too fast for me to understand.

Just then a truck with ten policemen—three in front, seven in the back—arrived from the nearby city of Esquinapa. Some had machine guns, others only rifles and pistols. They joined in the general merriment. If we'd had some beer and tacos we could have called it a picnic.

Then the police took the bomb and went away to some place where they are no doubt hammering and prying at it now. Cosme's hope for "Prrrrrraowh!" went with them.

The only point I want to make, and I trust President Reagan will see it immediately he reads this article, is that the global view of arms and armaments is not enough. Consideration should also be given to tiny parochial concerns about armaments.

It just may be that none of the banging is worth having, although in all honesty I must report we did have a lot of fun in this village for an hour or so. And there are grown men who share little Cosme's disappointment.

A Small and Quiet Place

|||

TEACAPAN—Ours is a quiet village, you understand. It isn't true but it's what we tell them. People have certain preconceptions which must be satisfied and the idea that a little Mexican village is quiet is one of those illusions.

A Mexican village is noisy. For instance, there are all those rockets. During the days before the celebration of the Virgin of Guadalupe, while shoals of little brown children float through the streets singing and carrying lighted candles on the palms of their hands, it is the custom to throw firecrackers and shoot rockets to the sky, setting all the dogs to barking.

At the celebration just concluded, some of the village's more devout religionists got heavily into the tequila one night and broke out the fireworks for the sainted lady at 4:00 A.M., filling the sky with whistles, hoots, screams, and magnificent explosions. Everybody here was able to participate in this celebration. Infants cried in their cribs, house parrots screamed in their cages, and all the dogs fought again on the streets.

It was almost as noisy as the next night when two neighbours in the block beside ours had a stereo war at 3:00 A.M. Almost everybody in the village has a stereo set. They may forego glass for the windows, using cement block fretwork instead, but they do not forego the stereo, music being the necessity of life that it is.

Being each possessed of powerful machines, the neighbours

took turns increasing the volume controls. The palm trees shook and the HOOWHEE creature ceased to shriek.

The HOOWHEE creature, as I call it, begins making this sound shortly after sunset and continues until dawn. I don't know if it is a reptile, a bird, or a ten-kilo insect. I have never seen it. I only hear it, repeating, repeating, repeating: HOOWHEE.

Fact is, the quiet of a Mexican village is not always easy to find, hour by hour, as our world turns.

The day begins here at 6:00 A.M. in the pink dawn when the loudspeaker on the church roof barks a few times. The priest then says: "Good morning, gentlemen, good morning, ladies," and invites us to Mass.

In Mexico one of the official revolutionary myths is that this is an atheist state, so priests and nuns are forbidden to appear on the streets in their religious clothing. Personally I would prefer to allow the priests to wear robes in the streets and prevent them from using loudspeakers at 6:00 A.M. But, then, it wasn't my revolution.

Throughout the day there will be loudspeakers beating us about the lugs. The clothing salesman in his Mexican-built Datsun van will boast of his exquisite quality and ruinously low prices as he travels, block by block. A big ten-wheeler may set up in the town square to sell blankets or cooking pots. The decibels of his speakers will be about equal to one of the heavier air raids on Hamburg.

We are never without iron-lunged street salesmen using loudspeakers. If, from time to time, they become hoarse and must visit the beer shop, they will set the things on music and leave them playing. In the evening, the movie house will put the sound track of its show on the loudspeaker. It will repeat the same sound track for as many nights as it keeps the movie. Many nights.

True, most of this electronic roaring is downtown. But downtown is so close in Teacapan. The village is 700 metres wide by 900 metres long.

Returning to the pearly morn, which we left at Mass, when the church bells will ring at least three times between 6:00 A.M. and 7:00 A.M., the next large and noticeable sound will be the arrival of the Norte de Sonora bus, a galleon of silver, scarlet, and gold.

Usually it will be unmufflered. There are few things a Mexican loves more than the straight-pipe exhaust.

Lest the machine-gun of the Norte de Sonora exhaust fails to excite the travellers, the driver will lean long on the world's most powerful air horn. Small birds will be knocked out of trees.

By 7:00 A.M. the farm tractors (unmufflered, what else?) are on their way to the fields. So are big trucks, carrying the farm hands.

At the beach the Yamaha outboards are thrumming, some being on boats coming home from a night of shark fishing, twelve miles offshore, and others on boats moving out for a day's fishing near the lagoon's mouth at the beach called Tambora. Tambora means drum, and you can hear the surf drumming on the shore sometimes when the village, in a fit of abstraction, falls silent for a moment or two.

Here, whistles blow all through the day. Why whistles? Why not whistles? They blow. That is all.

At the front gate a police whistle is blown by the boy who brings you your mail. In the schoolyards whistles are blown in the football and baseball games. People whistle.

There are stranger sounds. Burros don't whistle, but do their best to be noticed. Burros make free use of all our streets. They attend the church of their choice each Sunday. Sunday or any other day the males, when suffering from unrequited love, emit a raucous sound not quite matched this side of Hell.

When one of the desert canaries sings, most nearby dogs will bark and chase him or else turn to fighting one another. To fill any silences, the wild parakeets chitter, the sea birds shriek, and in at least half of the town's houses, stereos will play. In the other half, radios will play.

Mexican radio has picked up all of the worst habits of gringo commercial radio. Commercials are inflicted every three and one half minutes. Mexican radio people are particularly fond of the echo effect that can be obtained by shouting down a rain barrel.

The Mexican is by nature a quiet person. When he speaks his voice is low, gentle, rather musical. Why does he insist that everything that surrounds him be a thrashing, bashing, clashing concatenation of racket? Why do they hire brass bands for funerals? I'll tell you. I don't know.

There are also gentle sounds, even lovely ones. All Mexico sings. The fisherman, barefoot, packing a ten-horse outboard on his shoulder, sings as he comes down the street. The housewife, sweeping the mud floor of her home, sings. Workmen sing as they pack bricks and mix mortar. Children sing.

These people don't just hum or sing short snatches. They begin at the beginning and sing the song through to its end, the subject of the tale being, as a rule, unrequited love.

In our village, there is a quiet, of sorts, at the supper hour, except for unmuffled cars and motorcycles, stereos, TVs, radios, and the rolling thunder of voices from the beer parlour.

Also the town goes to bed early, as a town of farmers and fishermen must, if another day of grinding hard work is to be survived.

But each bedtime, as the yellow stars are set out on the black velvet blanket of the tropic sky, a new set of noises begins.

The land breeze now blows, and all the palm tree fronds clatter like dried bones being shaken. The burros sing. The dogs bark. The pigs—everybody has a pig—squeal. Pigs don't want to feel left out.

All through the night, the roosters crow.

A neighbour raises fighting cocks. Fighting cocks salute the dawn at 10:00 P.M. and keep it up all night. By the time dawn comes they are utterly exhausted, so they just quit and let dawn happen without them.

Our village's ordinary roosters—and everybody has that kind of rooster—also crow all night. They do it to signify that they could have been fighting cocks too, if it were not for deprived childhoods, which were no fault of theirs.

And the HOOWHEE creature takes up its cry. I have decided that it must be somebody preparing a television commercial. No reptile or insect could be so mindlessly repetitious.

You Can't Find a Thief
When You Need One

||||

TEACAPAN—If you want to know about Mexican crime, stay away from Mexico. The farther people are from here the more knowledgeably they talk about banditry.

In Canada, one house on our block was looted, wall to wall, while the family was away on a three-week vacation. When we leave our Canadian home we have someone else come to live in it. Yet here our house stands empty for slightly more than half of each year and nothing has ever been stolen.

Although not as confident as people far away to discuss the matter, we did have a bank robbery here the other day, so perhaps some personal observation of Mexican crime is now appropriate.

The two men with the gun got the bank's entire receipts of that day. But it was only noon, it's a small bank in a small village, so the loot amounted to the equivalent of only about $200 Canadian.

There is only one road connecting us to the Guadalajara highway. We might have expected a road blockade and Tommy-gun fire. But there was no fast getaway. There was no muscle car. Escape on saddle horse would have been colourful. That didn't happen either. In Chihuahua there are hot-blooded horses, but in Sinaloa horses are small and are said to sometimes fall asleep while making love.

Our bandits drove over to the lagoon in a Volkswagen Beetle. They pinched an outboard and were last seen headed towards San Blas. If they remembered to pack a case of beer and some shrimp, they had a pleasant picnic, because it was a sunny day but not oppressively hot.

Although interesting, this falls a little short of the Great Train Robbery or a million-dollar Brinks raid and please don't ask me to make it sound that big. I can't.

The only other current crimes of note here seem to be failure to make child support payments. For this, in Mexico, a man goes to jail. The authorities hold the view that if he won't pay support for his kids while he's out of jail and working for wages, then he might as well not support them while inside jail breaking rocks for the republic.

Oh well, you don't get the big picture of Mexican crime from a little village. I sought information from an acquaintance in Mazatlán. He is a gringo, in his fifties or sixties. Winter by winter, he has now accumulated several years of living in a Winnebago and sometimes in hotels and he drives huge motorcycles, the kind that have a stereo, a citizens' band radio, and an ice-making machine for the portable bar.

"Tell me about crime in Mexico," I said. "Because everybody knows it is rife."

"Its rifeness is not always apparent," he said. "I, personally, have put some effort into criminalizing the Mexicans and it has been a sore trial to me in my riper years."

"Tell me," I said. He did, and his story ran as follows:

The predecessor of his present Honda motorbike was, like the one he rides today, more powerful, more elaborate, and more expensive than many cars I have owned. Two years ago, owing to the oil shortage, he fried the camshaft. The big machine purred like the tiger it was, but the gringo knew that its heart needed expensive surgery.

"Looking at the bill I faced, looking at the machine, which was still worth a good $4,500 U.S., it was clear that the path of prudence was to have it stolen so I could collect the insurance."

He drove to Juárez at the Texas border. Juárez may not be the toughest of the border towns, but it will do for an example.

The gringo knew a man of the world who dwelt in Juárez. He told this man that, should some reliable criminals be sent his way, he had information that might appeal to them.

"Three men turned up. I explained I needed to have a motor-cycle stolen.

"We went to a section of Juárez about five blocks from the border crossing, an unlovely side of town. 'I will leave it here,' I said. 'The key will be just under this little pillion seat. There's lots of gas. Would six hours be enough to do the job?'

"They said six hours was plenty. I walked across the border to the U.S. and got a motel room. Six hours later I walked back. The bike was still at the curb.

"I left it there, went back to the U.S. side, and slept. I came to the Mexican side next day. The machine hadn't moved.

"I hunted up the three thieves. They said there had been some delays but all was well now. They knew a policeman who loved big Hondas and they were sure he would pay handsomely. I told them: 'I don't care if you sell it to your mother-in-law or to the president of Mexico or the president of the United States. I don't want any money from you. All I want is for that machine to dis-appear so that neither I nor the insurance company ever see it again.' They promised it would be taken from me. Typical Mexi-cans. Tell you what they think you want to hear."

On the next day he found the Honda still at the curb, shining in the sun but not quite so brightly now, for the street dust was settling heavily upon it.

"I figured it out. The thieves were convinced I was setting them up for the police.

"What I could not understand was where all the other profes-sional and amateur criminals of Mexico were. That machine stood on a badly lit street of a slum area. Anybody could have found the keys, or wired the ignition, or bundled it into a truck, or just walked it down the street.

"In New York, a Winnebago would have been gutted overnight and left, no wheels, no engine, no drivetrain, for the wreckers to pack away. I tried to park overnight on Wall Street once and a New York policeman told me I'd be on the curb in my pyjamas before morning, looking at the husk of what used to be a motor home. That is, if I was still healthy enough to look. He told me to get the machine behind guarded walls somewhere.

"But a Honda bike in Juárez? No way.

"Do you know the end of the story? Yes, I perceive that you do. At the end of the six days and nights, nobody had got off his ass to steal my beautiful big bike. I got fed up with paying U.S. motel bills and I took it home, where the repairs cost me a lot of money."

The gringo and I agreed that Mexican crime isn't always as advertised.

Cutting Tile
and Breaking Custom

|||

TEACAPAN—When I was a child and too small to be worth anything much, there were still steam shovels in Canada, primitive earth-moving machines that smoked and hissed impressively and performed what then seemed to be heroic tasks of construction.

My grandfather used a steam shovel to give economic direction to my green and pliant mind: A man watching a steam shovel said to the operator, "Instead of you, just one man, being employed here with this machine, there could be a hundred men, using shovels."

The steam shovel operator answered, "Right you are. Or a thousand men, using teaspoons."

Here it is 1986, Mexico, and my neighbour Elias confronts the same old dilemma.

Elias is a big, gentle man, slow of motion, slow of speech, slow to laugh, and slow to anger. He has the reputation of being scrupulously honest, so I suppose you could also say he is slow to cheat.

Elias cuts and lays ceramic tile for a living. He's a maestro. His earnings are not grand. The minimum daily wage for such a maestro is about $9.25 Canadian. On this he must support a wife and four small children.

Last year Elias tiled a patio table and a section of wall for us. The work was done perfectly, but to watch him do it was to weep.

For cutting ceramic tiles, Elias had three rotten little tools. One was a slice of metal that may have been a broken saw blade. At its tip there was one tooth of carbide steel. With this he would score a tile for cutting, working from the clay side, not the glazed side, until the tile was almost severed.

He next used his second tool, which was half a hacksaw blade. With this he scored each edge of his tile cut.

He then broke the tile, almost always successfully, and finally used his third tool, a large, rusty file, to smooth the rough edges of the break.

Unnoticed by Elias, I timed him. To cut a little 110-mm-square ornamental tile took him five minutes and twenty seconds. At home in Canada I have cut forty tiles in as many minutes, using a simple score-and-snap tile cutter.

Elias was two days putting tile on our table and our wall. The job was worth half a day in time, at the most. However, Elias charged so little for his time that we profited by hiring him.

This year I bought a tile cutter for Elias while passing through the United States. It has a long arm, a wheel like a glass cutter's, a table marked out in inches, and an arm for snapping the scored tile cleanly. The cost was $50 U.S., which was $69.50 Canadian.

When Elias dropped around to say hello, I offered him the machine in exchange for work on our house. I demonstrated it for him. He had never seen one, although he had heard of them. He tried it, mastered it in a minute, liked it, and called it truly and remarkably practical. He has taken it home.

So far, this may seem to represent the onward and upward movement of technology.

But does it?

Elias now faces the old problem of adapting technological change to people, and people, contrary devils that they are, never seem ready for improvement.

For as long as he has worked, Elias has never done a job as a package contract. Never has he looked at what needs to be done and offered a firm price for doing it. He follows custom, charging by the day. He may estimate the probable total cost, but he will not guarantee it. Indeed, much of the modest success of Elias's tile business rests on the fact that he is known to be honest and not one who spins work out for extra money.

With the new tile cutter, it is hard to see how Elias can follow that system. Instead of cutting one tile in five minutes, he will be cutting eight tiles in one minute. To charge a daily rate for his work, work which he will finish in so much less time, could ruin him.

Simple, says the American or Canadian. Let Elias now charge by the job instead of by the day.

It's not that simple. This is still a village, ruled by customs.

If Elias changes to a fixed contract price, who will believe his price? Why should they? Why did he change the custom of charging by the day?

People will say: "He was here half a day and charged me for two days of work."

No problem, says the Canadian or the American. Elias will be more competitive. He will get the jobs that other tile layers do not get, because his final price will be lower. Thank you so much, Adam Smith.

Things are not that way here.

There are not many tiling jobs in Teacapan. Elias and three or four other maestros can do them all. If Elias got every job, thus earning the enduring enmity of all the other tile-layers and their wives, in-laws, and godfathers, he would be no better off than if he were continuing to charge by the day instead of by the job. And he could not expand his business to neighbouring towns or villages. His only transportation is a bicycle, and a car is as far beyond his financial capacity as a Cessna 185 on floats.

In this community, Elias gets his share of the work with the reputation of being slow, sure, and fair.

The patented score-and-snap tile cutter is not slow and, like a steam shovel, it knows nothing about fairness, one way or the other. I don't know what Elias will do with the cutter. I don't think he does either.

¡Faith in God and Advance!

|||

OBREGON, SONORA—It has been suggested I write about driving in Mexico before it is too late.

The situation here is best summed up by the old Spanish battle cry that one will see from time to time, painted in scarlet and gold lettering on the back of badly beat-up cars: "*Fe en Dios, y adelante.*"

Not all sayings retain their musical cadence in translation, but this one does: "Faith in God and advance!"

All Mexican traffic advances utmostly. It is not hindered by fear or by formal traffic regulation. In this country everybody has a right to go anywhere, to Hell for instance, at the pace he chooses.

However, this can make for dreadful clutter, because the traffic is so varied.

On the highways, most trucks and cars are new, shiny, Mexican-made Fords, Volkswagens, Nissans, Dodges, and other vehicles familiar to the gringo eye. There are also Greyhound-type buses and legions of modern trucks. Mixed with these, however, are trucks and cars that have survived, although barely, for ten, twenty, and thirty years of hardship and abuse. These walking wounded move not much faster than grey, sun-beaten old wooden carts hitched to two little burros.

There are also farm tractors, not all of which display lights. There are unescorted burros, dogs, and herds of goats; there are motorcyclists, bicyclists, and pedestrians. There are buzzards eating the travellers who have been unlucky.

The burros, the Greyhound buses, the Chrysler New Yorkers, and the 1949 Chevs all have equal rights on these roads, and every single driver knows it. Therefore, to participate in Mexican traffic is quite a bit of fun, provided you do not kill yourself.

There are a few traffic laws, doubtless, but all pale into insignificance beside the one primary law—it is against the law to have a motor vehicle accident. Provided you do not have an accident, you may drive pretty much as you please.

There is a law of right of way that is helpful to know. It is the same as the law for sailboats. The vehicle whose fender protrudes an inch or two past another vehicle's is the one with the right of way.

Should you wish to overtake a car on the right and cross over in front of it to the left, just do that very thing. It is up to the other driver to take evasive action. If he doesn't he will be reminded of the saying "He who hits pays."

As you will observe in city traffic, left and right turn signals are not usually used. That is because they just tip off the other driver to your intentions and you wouldn't want him to know them, would you?

What happens if you wheel a Volkswagen into the path of a Greyhound bus? Why, dear chap, the bus rolls right over the Volkswagen and demolishes it. But one does not challenge a big vehicle with a small one because here common sense overrides all laws and all traditions.

The substitution of common sense for law and regulation is one of the significant differences between Mexican drivers and gringo drivers.

Americans and Canadians believe that you always proceed on a green traffic light and always stop for a red one. They think that's written into their national constitutions.

The Mexican believes that red and green lights are designed to help the traffic move across intersections. Therefore, at 2:00 A.M. on a city street when there is no traffic crossing on a green light, the Mexican driver crosses on the red and thinks nothing of it.

(The pedestrian traffic lights of home, which we tend to unthinkingly obey even on empty streets, are not known in Mexico. You should not talk to Mexicans about them. It only reinforces their suspicion that everybody dwelling north of the Rio Grande is completely mad.)

In all traffic, then, the equal rights of some are more equal than those of others.

Once in Mexico City a traffic policeman on point duty was asked why he waved big, speeding limousines through red lights on the busy Reforma Boulevard, where they scattered all the green-light cars and pedestrians like quail as they roared through.

"Those are generals," he said.

"How can you tell they are generals?"

"I can smell them."

This helps here, a sense of smell or some kind of second sight. It may enable you to anticipate the car that is coming at you full throttle, in your lane, on a blind corner in the mountains. (He has flashed his headlights to establish right of way, something which will give you both great comfort in the next world.)

As for driving the highways by night, among half-lit and unlit farm vehicles, burros, stray horses, and zebu cows, nobody should do it until he has paid off the mortgage, provided for a full college education for all his kids, and set up adequate funds for his widow.

But even by daylight, what is it, other than an illuminated plastic Jesus on the dashboard, that keeps the average driver alive here?

The statistics I do not know. I wouldn't believe them if they were offered. I don't entirely believe highway accident statistics at home, where everybody is insured and where all auto body repairmen are licensed. I can only state, from a number of years sharing these roads with Mexicans, that one observes no more collisions and upsets than in British Columbia.

The Mexican system, anarchy, is not all bad. Everybody on these streets and roads, burros and goats excepted, remembers at all times that he has a responsibility to avoid accidents and the unwelcome attention of authorities which comes with accidents. The Mexican driver is often wild, he may be wilful, he is never unaware. The traffic advances.

The Revolution,
God and Santa Claus

|||

TEACAPAN—Between our arrival here in mid-November and year's end, four major festivals will have interrupted life in this village. Nothing of note will have been accomplished. Remember that. No accomplishment.

The celebrations will have cost more than the people can afford. Most people here are hard put to afford food. By ordinary standards, they can't afford anything for fun and games. But, then, here as elsewhere, life is not always rational. Remember that also.

The fiestas, in order of their appearance, are Revolution Day, Day of Christ the King, the fiesta of the Virgin of Guadalupe, and Christmas.

Christmas you will know something about. The others you may not be familiar with.

Revolution Day is called by its date: Twentieth of November. That was the day in 1910 when the upheaval began. The revolution was to last two decades and cost two and a half million lives.

These people were trying to break the power of the oligarchy, including the Roman Catholic Church. They wanted to give land to the peasants and education to the poor. They subscribed to all the contradictory slogans of any revolution in which liberty and equality, the two irreconcilables, are included.

Ever since, Mexico has been governed as a one-party state that uses democratic forms. The rulers call themselves the Party of the Institutionalized Revolution and parades on November 20 seem to be one of the institutions.

Not a single veteran of the revolutionary war remains in this village. The last of them was a fine old gentleman who, when I met him, was in his eighties and still went daily to work in the bean fields. "If I am still around when you come back, remember that my house is your house," he said. But he wasn't still around when I came back.

Now the parade is composed entirely of schoolchildren and junior college students. Since these make up more than half the population of Teacapan, the front of the parade almost catches up to the back of the parade in a twenty-block circuit of the town.

Squad by squad the kids march by, all sparkling clean in a village that is not.

One class carries basketballs, another gym poles, another balloons, another paper streamers. Girls come dressed as Red Cross nurses. Boys from physical fitness classes perform acrobatics.

The contingent of the small children, those who can barely keep up with the march, is the only one in which boys and girls march together. Before puberty, it's apparently considered safe.

The little girls are dressed in 1910 period costume. The boys have imitation bandoleers strapped over their shoulders. They carry toy guns or air rifles. Moustaches are painted on their faces. The boys are not hard to recognize. They are tiny replicas of Emiliano Zapata who, until Che Guevera came along, was the most romantic and handsome of all Marxist revolutionary heroes.

All this, in memory of what nobody now remembers.

Since Francisco Madero started the great revolution, the Mexican people have been robbed blind by a succession of bad governments. Rulers who didn't rob them mismanaged their economy so badly that they might as well have used pistols. The verdict isn't in yet on the de la Madrid government, but it is the same old party. In this country, only God knows how Mexico can ever pay its way out of a bankruptcy that is so much more apparent and undeniable than the Canadian and American government bankruptcies.

So what do these neat, trim, and rather charming kids parade for? It can be asked also about the other festivals.

The Day of Christ the King celebrates the holy patron whom fishermen claim for their own. Many children of fishing families are named Jesus.

In Teacapan the Christo Rey fiesta begins at 4:00 A.M. with the firing of rockets in the village plaza. Having ensured that nobody can sleep and that the population will take another needless jump nine months hence, Teacapan is kept awake and moving for the rest of a long day. By nightfall, the plaza is awash with people large and small and there are frequent firings of a type of firecracker called The Snake, which darts around at ankle height throwing sparks and flame. These inflict first-degree burns, without which it wouldn't seem like a real fiesta.

How well the patron saint has cared for fisher folk this year is another matter.

The summer rains failed to come. There were heat waves. The sun, people say, came down.

Men, women, and children paraded, day by day, praying for the rains. In this furnace the waters of the big lagoon heated and almost all the shrimp died. Made desperate, the lagoon fishermen took their little boats into the open ocean. That was an invasion of the trawlers' territory. The trawlers demanded action by fishery patrol officers. There were arrests and seizures of Teacapan fishermen's gear. Animosities have been aroused that will not be calmed for a long time.

But you would not know this to see the district shut up shop in midweek for celebration of Christ the King Day.

In the first part of December, we celebrate the Feast of the Virgin of Guadalupe. Each night as darkness falls, young and old march the streets, singing and carrying lighted candles in the palms of their hands. There is always at least one section of paraders dressed as Indians. The Virgin, Mexico's patron saint, is classified as Indian.

As usual, more firecrackers. We shall be lucky if we pass the next three weeks without at least one little boy losing a finger or two in proving that he can hold a Roman candle longer than anybody else before releasing it. Such scars are like duelling scars at Heidelberg University, honourable, for some reason.

And then comes Christmas, which sets all the poverty and the richness of Mexican life side by side.

The poverty, of course, isn't hard to find. It's there in the poor, ill-dressed woman from a village in the mountains who is buying at a Mazatlán department store. She cannot read nor write nor figure so she scoops up all the clothes and toys she would like to have, knowing that neither God nor the store plans on her having them all.

She carries these to the checkout, piles them on a counter and beside them lays her pitiful little pile of pesos. The checkout girl has been through this many times. She first discards dresses and toys of which any single one has a price higher than the peasant woman's entire stock of money. Then to the smaller items, keeping this one for the store, giving that one to the village woman. Finally, when there is only a tiny pile remaining, the girl takes the money and rings it into the cash machine.

The woman from the village is as uncomplaining as she is uncomprehending. This is the way of the new, great and rich Mexican economy on whose outer edge she lives. She takes her little handful and goes.

I have no way of calculating how many children in our village will get a present this Christmas, but probably more than in Christmases past. The essence of the holiday here has been changing. Traditionally, presents were only given on the twelfth day after Christmas. They were called the gifts of the Three Kings and they were almost always small. However, Sinaloa is one of the northern states and subject to stronger American influences than most of Mexico. Now Christmas Day is becoming the day for presents, if presents are affordable, and Santa Claus replaces the Three Kings in shop windows.

Despite these changes, Christmas here remains a fiesta which chiefly resembles American and Canadian Thanksgiving Days, with a touch of Easter. As with Easter, this is a time of the great ingathering of the clans.

The highways are stiff with cars and busses carrying Mexican people home, home from California, home from Texas, home from Guadalajara, Mexico City and the oil fields of the Yucatan. This is the richness of Mexican life—the warmth and the life-giving power of family.

That, and the firm and seemingly incontrovertible conviction that our life on this earth demands that we celebrate it from time to time, whether or not we can afford to do so.

Irreverence
and a Swaggering Gallantry
|||

TEACAPAN—Most of the little band of soldiers with which Cortés conquered Mexico were Andalusians from the arid and wretchedly poor south of Spain. William Lytle Schurz, author of the book *This New World,* offers this description of the Andalusian character: "[They] distinguished themselves by their quick wit and resourcefulness and a certain swaggering gallantry, as well as by their irresponsible ways and their refusal to accept the official version of anything as the gospel truth."

Mr. Schurz possesses second sight or is the seventh son of a seventh son, because his words have an uncanny quality. True, he is speaking in generalities, and all generalities are false (including this one). But if you spend any time in this country you cannot easily dismiss an analysis like Mr. Schurz's because it fits, so very closely, the apparent characteristics of the Mexicans living today, four and a half centuries after the conquest.

It can't be in the blood. The Andalusian strain is spread thin among the 75 million modern Mexicans, particularly in this little village of farmers and fishermen in Sinaloa State.

Those are not characteristics taught in the schools. In modern Mexican history books, Cortés has become almost a nonperson. It is said that in the whole republic there is not a single monument to the conqueror.

If there is a reason for modern Mexicans to resemble the *conquistadores,* I leave it to others to explain. I report what I observe.

". . . distinguished themselves by their quick wit and resourcefulness . . ."

Any Mexican who has learned to breathe has learned to laugh. He laughs a great deal of the time. Some might say that there are times when he should cry instead, but he can't hear these people because he is laughing.

An example is the tractor operator who capsized his machine, his livelihood, in our driveway. He was not killed, but he plainly heard the rustle of angels' wing feathers.

Within half an hour three other tractors pulled up to help and remained to make jokes. We all had some beer and brandy. "Fiesta Mexicana," I said. That's not particularly witty but they appreciate a gringo trying to be funny and everybody, including the poor man with the wrecked tractor, gave it a good round of laughter.

Our washerwoman's little boy wept the other morning because his school class was making a bus trip that day and he could not go because he had no shoes to wear. Our washerwoman lives through a lot of experiences such as that. I have scarcely ever met a person to whom laughter comes so readily, so spontaneously.

She has a keen eye for human frailty and human pomposity but these do not anger her. They make her laugh. She makes other people laugh. She can give to human foolishness an endearing quality with the turn of her tongue.

Some Mexican wit, like Jewish wit, may be mordant, particularly if it be applied to government. But it is good stuff. "The Mexican economy recovers every night, while the government people are sleeping."

As for resourcefulness, the Mexicans are like the Russians, of whom Nikita Khrushchev said: "I have a nation of 250 million magicians who live at 1,000 rubles a month on a 500-ruble-a-month salary."

At time of writing, minimum wage for day labour in Mexico is 850 pesos. An average family, which here is about six people, needs at least 1,500 pesos a day to eat. Some say 2,000 pesos a day.

There are examples of poverty quite staggering to gringos.

Thanks, no doubt, to government subsidies, you can obtain

enough natural gas to cook and heat water for a household for a full month for the equivalent of $2.50 Canadian. Yet, daily, old dugout canoes are paddled across the water to the swamplands of the nearby state of Nayarit and they return loaded with firewood, which men, women, and children pack on their backs to houses which have no glass in the windows. The wood is wet and burns poorly, as do also the coconut husks, but if you cannot afford $2.50 a month for natural gas, that is what you burn.

Obviously beneath the abundant evidence of poverty there is an ability for survival that the economists can never quite explain to us.

In this dusty little community, it is rare that children do not go daily, cheerful and seemingly well fed, to their schools.

On Mondays, almost every child goes in uniform: clean white shirts, clean khaki or blue pants. Mondays are the days Mexican children honour their flag, their country, and the revolution.

". . . and a certain swaggering gallantry . . ."

The Mexican may be in rags and barefoot. In a little backwater community like ours his Spanish may be peppered with Indian words and mangled badly by slang. He may know remarkably little about anything that is more than fifty kilometres from his village. But he does know who he is. He is his own man, and proud of it.

He makes it quite clear that he is as good a man as you are. Privately, he is convinced that he is a much better man, but politeness forbids him from saying so. His manners are almost invariably courtly.

Mexicans are not good sanitation experts. They are horrid plumbers. They can misuse, neglect, and otherwise spoil good machinery faster than it can be manufactured. But their manners are exquisite. They are a classy people.

". . . as well as by their irresponsible ways . . ."

A Canadian lady, living part of each year in nearby Gringo Gulch, had a tire on her Volkswagen go flat. She hurried to the nearest garage and asked that it be fixed.

This was a day just before a Mexican national holiday. Down

here, many days come just before or just after Mexican national holidays.

The mechanic walked around the car and looked carefully at each tire.

"Dear lady, you are mistaken. There is air in all the tires."

"It's the spare that is flat," she said.

His usual courtesy deserted him. He told her to go away and return, if she still insisted on returning, two days later.

Almost all Mexicans understand why their car manufacturers put a fifth tire in all the cars they make. They know it is a spare. But they consider it damned degrading to carry one. When they can afford a new car one of their first actions is to flog the extra tire for beer money, thus relieving themselves of insult and God Almighty of a certain degree of discourtesy.

Frugality may be imposed upon the Mexican by hard realities but at least he may avoid prudence by his own initiative.

Spare tire stories are funny. Other stories of improvidence are not. In our community there are very poor families who borrowed money from the bank recently during the pre-Lenten fiesta so that they might have beer for themselves and candy for their children.

". . . and their refusal to accept the official version of any-thing . . ."

Half the Americans don't vote any more. A quarter of the Canadians don't and their numbers may well grow. But in Mexico disillusionment is far more profound.

These people appear to no longer feel either anger or despair about government. They have come to view it as an affliction, like aging, and, like aging, it must eventually kill us all.

No one can suggest that Mexican governments have been pure. To say that there has been extensive graft and corruption is to do no more than repeat the words of the present Mexican government which is, at this time, trying to extradite some alleged grafters of the previous regime from the United States and Canada.

But if this little community be any example, it won't matter how much or how little the Miguel de la Madrid government effects reforms. Cynicism can be, like ignorance, invincible.

Now and then a Mexican acquaintance will tell us: "What we need is another Pancho Villa."

Only Villa, Zapata, Madero, Juárez, Father Hidalgo, and a few other political figures are dead enough to be honoured here. But if any one of these mythic heroes could be reconstituted and restored to the governing of Mexico, it is hard to believe that he would long command public confidence.

Personally, I would not choose to be an honest politician in this land. Why bother? It is expensive and it surprises and disappoints the masses.

Where there is no hope, it is said, the people perish. But remember that the hope the Mexican has lost is the hope of good government. He still has those other qualities, the wit, the resourcefulness, the grace, and the gallantry. In those things, which are himself, he has faith.

Wolf Man Meets Skinned Rabbit

|||

TEACAPAN—An excellent magazine named *Texas Highways*, which should know better, recently ran an article on Texas nicknames. We learned that a man who bought a popcorn field was called Popcorn and that another with a peg leg was called—can you guess?—Pegleg.

This shows that the Mexicans should have kept Texas, if only to improve the English of the Texans.

Mexicans are not imaginative when bestowing names at a christening. The same old ones are repeated over and over again. Arturo and Alfredo. Juan, Jesus and José. Maria and Magdalena. ·Rafael. Victor. These, it seems, never change. But that is because the parents, the in-laws and all the friends in the neighbourhood are waiting to see something different, something new and refreshing in this particular child of the great republic.

When they do—and they will take their time about it—other people will put one hand to an ear to listen to it, to see if it is witty and if it rings true. If it passes, it may become, in many ways, more important than the original and legal name. Nicknames may change, and some do, but others last unto the grave, even though they are never chiselled into the tombstone.

It is a system with some resemblance to that of Indians in the north of the continent. In most tribes a person's name changed as he or she entered different phases of life. One might have one name as an infant, another as an adolescent, a third as a chief and a fourth or fifth after experiencing visions. As life changed—

and whose life does not?—a name should also change. The notion that parents could select a name for an infant which would serve for a whole lifetime was considered absurd.

The Mexican system differs from this in that the nicknames are created for fun. They tend to be just a bit sly. They have, like good chilis, an afterburn.

Nicknames in Teacapan will do for samples.

A fat man is not called Fatty. He is called Doublewide.

An apparently rich man who has built a handsome estate on the beach, a man who travels accompanied by hard-eyed bodyguards, rejoices in the name The Crazy Pig.

A neighbour named Juan, who has a vestigial sixth toe on one foot, is called Twenty-one John. It's true, it's bright, it's to-the-point, and it is distinctive.

There can be lots of Shorties, Big Noses, and Limpys in a town (to quote from that Texas magazine) but few are likely to have more than one Twenty-one John.

Another John drives a taxi, and almost always his trip is forty kilometres to the city of Esquinapa and then forty kilometres back to Teacapan.

He is, to use the Spanish, Juan Vuelta, pronounced Wan Welta. Good nicknames often add alliteration to their charm. It means Turnaround John.

A nickname may even be collectively held. There is an old couple often seen together on the streets, both very tall, very thin, and very straight. They are called Eleven.

Gringos are not exempted from the nicknaming and take what they get. One, who had pop eyes, a long nose, and was given to jerky arm movements, was named Pinocchio.

He did not much like Mexicans nor did they like him, so the name had particular significance. If slurred, in Spanish, the word Pinocchio becomes almost indistinguishable from the word for a portion of the human anatomy on which the sun does not shine. Nicknames don't just happen. People work at them.

My wife, who is small and frequently rides her horse beside the waves on the beach, is called Beach Bird.

I am sometimes known as Wolf Man, which arises, I am told, because there is hair on my muzzle, my eyes are pale, and I have a habit of restless walking.

Nicknames last long, and many are permanent.

One neighbour, now in middle age, went to a neighbouring region to work as a field hand when a teen-ager and returned with jaundice. To this day, he is called Nanchie, which is the name of a small yellow fruit.

Not far from him lives a fisherman who got very drunk one night, as fishermen sometimes do, stripped off all his clothes, and sat on the street with his head and arms resting on his knees.

In that position he reminded somebody of a skinned rabbit and to this day, some fifteen years later, he is called Skinned Rabbit.

When it comes to nicknames Texans should not try to compete in the Mexican league. They are outgunned.

Stereotypes,
Since You Insist

|||

TEACAPAN—Somebody has accused me of being in love with the Mexicans. Might as well bow my back and take the blow, I suppose.

In truth, I find Mexicans pretty much like other people. Some are great, some so-so, and some are not worth the powder to blow them to Hell. Or, as the great Ambrose Bierce said, "In every man there is a tiger, a pig, an ass, and a nightingale."

However, nations and nationalities do have prominent characteristics. There are ways by which the Mexican is known, or, if not known, then recognized.

As a bunch, as a stereotype if you will, Mexicans have good manners. They smile a lot. They like to sing. They laugh a great deal. They work hard. They are by nature honest and hospitable.

There I go again, liking Mexicans, even though it be only the liking for a stereotype.

I shall reform. I shall talk about Mexican characteristics I do not like.

For instance, if given a choice, I would never hire a Mexican plumber. It would not matter if he had won international awards for the delicacy with which he wiped a soldered joint or the artistry with which he built a tiled, sunken bathtub. If I knew him to be Mexican, or even half-Mexican, I would not hire him. A Mexican plumber is like an English cook or a German police officer.

I love not the dirt of Mexico, nor the flies, nor the garbage that litters the streets.

In a grocery store in our village, flies are like flocks of pigeons. The floor appears to get swept only once a week.

The local butcher hangs his meat on a rack on the sidewalk. The dust of passing trucks cakes it, flies devour it, and the dogs snatch at it.

I do not like the inefficiency of Mexico and nobody has yet convinced me that it is charming and therefore admirable.

In the few supermarkets that are available in the cities, the kids at the checkout could have been trained to read the price on one can of refried beans and then multiply that price by the number of cans. But no, each identical can is scrutinized individually.

The check to see if your credit card is good is agonizingly long, apparently because the list of bad credit cards is like a dictionary, it has so many entries. How could anybody be expected to find any single word in it? The clerks pretend to check for bad credit cards and then give up.

My bank has paid other people's electricity bills from my account and then, perhaps by way of apology, credited other people's deposits to my account. Once it sent some private papers of mine to a gringo in Arizona.

When I taxed the bank manager with this error—a Paul St. Pierre in Fort Langley is not like a Sam Cox in Tubac—he said I should pay no attention, it was merely a mistake. By calling it a mistake he had offered a full and complete Mexican explanation. No further investigation or consideration of the matter was required, either by me or by him.

In matters sexual, Mexican men tend to make horses' asses of themselves when around women. An example is one in this village who became concerned about his potency. The Mexican male seems to spend much of his life worrying about this.

The man left his wife and took up with a young girl. She used birth control. He pleaded, he insisted she cease to do so. She ceased and when she became pregnant, he immediately left her and returned to his wife, who welcomed him home as all good Mexican women are taught to do.

Mexican men are raised in the belief that they are God's gift to the ladies. It is easy to believe the reports that they are the clumsiest of amateurs when in bed.

I do not like the way Mexicans treat animals. Their dogs die young from malnutrition and their horses and mules, although more useful than the dogs, do about as badly.

One may sympathize with the Mexicans' poverty without approving the ways in which they recklessly aggravate it. Typically, a Mexican treats machinery as he does his animals: he uses it hard, gives not an instant to its care and maintenance, and then throws it away before a normal lifetime is attained.

A youngster nearby, of an extremely poor family, was given a well-constructed, brand-new bicycle two years ago. It now looks as if it had been thrown out of an airplane. The boy's mother excuses him. After all, she says, what can you expect, it is an old bicycle.

So far I have not dealt with the popular gringo beliefs that Mexicans are bandits, that you are not safe outside a high-rise American-style hotel, and that, as health insurance salespeople will gladly inform you, you will be forever bankrupt if you must ever enter a Mexican hospital. But the first two of these allegations seem absurdly improbable when you live here, and the third is an absolute untruth.

But, then, there will be those who read my stereotyped criticisms on this page and disagree with all of them. There is no pleasing some people.

Friendly But Not Married

|||

GUADALAJARA, JALISCO—On a winter night, when snow was falling on the Mother Mountains, when the wind on the Guadalajara Plain was dry and cold as old white bones among the cactus, we drove late into this city with no motel reservations.

In many decades of travel I have almost always arrived in cities without reservations and have scarcely ever found them necessary or desirable. However, this story had to begin somehow and that is the way I'm beginning it. Would you have preferred: "It was a dark and stormy night. The brigands sat around the campfire . . ."? No? Well then, we came late into Guadalajara without reservations.

We drove a lot of dark streets in strange neighbourhoods and missed death scantly half a dozen times from the world's second fastest drivers. They are not quite so fast here as in Mexico City. Then we came upon a softly lit motel called Venus which had a star on its spire. Here was haven for the homeless, rest for the weary, ease for the troubled.

I drove through the gate, past a wicket with a middle-aged lady at a cash register, and entered the underground parking area. The stalls for cars had curtains. A deft touch, I thought. First we have motels built as separate units, now we have motels with a private garage for every car.

Only a couple of these had the curtains drawn back and the stall empty. We could see that from the parking space a circular stairway led to what were presumably the motel rooms upstairs.

The route through the car park led us back to the wicket and its friendly although somewhat dowdy attendant. I said we wanted a room for the night.

"A whole night?" she said.

I have always had the seat about four rows from the front in the slow learners' class. Yes, I said, we wanted it all the night and most of the morning too.

"Sir," she said, "this establishment is for people who are friendly."

Well, we are like any other married couple. We have our good days and our bad days, but most people who know us think we get along fairly well. We might argue a bit, but there wouldn't be any furniture broken. I was trying to arrange some of my forty-seven words of Spanish to put this all in perspective for the lady but while I was sorting she spoke again.

"This is for people who are friendly but who are not married."

We were tempted to stay anyway, although the rates, being hourly, were high and the only room service was lots of towels and sheets.

What did happen is that Auntie at the Gate directed us to El Tapatio. Although it later deteriorated, El Tapatio, at that time, rated as a grand hotel.

I have little affection for grand hotels. My preference is for what are called motels, preferably built as separate cottages, each with a carport where I may wheel in with my riceburner, packing my own bags, cooking my own coffee, and leaving at whatever hour of the next morning with the bill already paid. However, there are exceptions to my low and vulgar tastes.

I have known grand hotels that lived up to the name. Seldom. But I have.

The greatest in my memory remains the Peninsular in Kowloon where I learned that it is possible for an establishment to be run on the principle that every guest deserves to be treated like royalty. The Savoy on the banks of the Thames can make the same claim. El Tapatio is the third and pretty well the last big hotel for which I have felt any sentiment that could be graced with the word affection.

It is more motel than hotel, being a series of terraces laid upon one of the hills that overlook the city of Guadalajara. This is one of the few inns at which the bellboy leads you to your room in his own Volkswagen, winding up the cobbled streets, past the cages where the lions lay sleeping that night when we first came there, and out, finally, to the promontory of that rocky hill where your quarters are.

In Vancouver, Tapatio would be terraced apartments occupying all of Little Mountain but retaining the arboretum.

Here, each room has a balcony hung with flowers from which you can look over all of the great city but from which you cannot see the guest who uses the balcony next door.

On that cold night of long ago there was fresh fruit in the bowls, liquor in the cabinet, fruit juice in the refrigerator. There was no tipping, which suited me, since I consider tipping an abomination that should have been eliminated at about the same time as the Inquisition.

The next morning my wife and I found other things about Tapatio we liked. There were horses to rent, shops with eelskin handbags, and a swimming pool large enough to have an island in the centre where waiters, using a small causeway, brought you drinks in hollowed-out pineapples. There was a separate play area for noisy children.

Although I need shuffleboard and tennis about as much as I need Wheaties and Poopsies for breakfast, it was nice to know that shuffleboard, tennis, golf, and dancing lessons were available. It wasn't entirely offensive that Wheaties and Poopsies were available, together with decent Mexican-style breakfasts in the cafeteria.

And it all cost the equivalent of $75 Canadian.

El Tapatio was an experiment which ultimately didn't quite work. Tipping was reintroduced. In later years prices went up and service went down. Some of the hotel rooms were sold as condominiums and cockroaches found their way into the bathrooms.

But on that cold and windy night it was for us the pavilion of Paradise.

The woman at the desk, filling out one of those multiple-answer survey forms, wanted to know how we had heard about Tapatio. I told her we were sent by the place that sells love by the hour.

Pistachios and Propriety

|||

TEACAPAN—My wife stuck a forefinger in my ear and rotated it, a sign that she wanted me to remember some instruction for longer than it took for her to tell it.

"When you go to the store tell Lucilla I can't take her to town today for the nuts; I've got too much to do here at the house."

"What's this about nuts?"

"She wanted a ride to town to pick up a sack of nuts which are there for her, but I'm too busy."

"I'm not busy," I said.

"How true . . ."

"So I'll throw on a clean shirt and run her to town."

"Maybe," said my wife. She grew up a member of the new bilingual generation of Texas and sometimes has insights into the Mexican character that escape me.

I was back home ten minutes later.

"Lucilla couldn't go today after all," I said.

"Fancy that," said my wife.

Later she and Lucilla had one of those woman-to-woman discussions, which women have with women, if you follow me. A man has to be married awhile before he learns that his wife discusses his private habits with a frankness and fullness quite alien to the male nature. Men are by nature prudes. Women are by nature whatever is the word for the opposite of prude.

Lucilla, it seems, raised the matter of my assault upon her

virtue, and my wife, I regret tremendously to report, said that I was really quite harmless.

"He just had time on his hands and thought he'd run you into Esquinapa for the pistachios. He really didn't plan to get you into bed, Lucilla."

"Oh, really?" said Lucilla. "Then why was it the only time I have ever seen him clean?"

These are terrible libels. I do occasionally go to Lucilla's store in my surf-fishing pants and an old shirt, but I am frequently there freshly shaven. However, Lucilla's remark delighted my spouse such as nothing since the last shoe sale. "I told her that even though you were clean, you were not bent on rapine."

"In the name of God," I said, "what country are we in? What century is this?"

"Well, my dear, it has some similarity to Camelot, and that was about a thousand years ago."

"Teacapan? Camelot!"

"You have got to see it from her point of view. As she says, this is a small town and everybody talks. She put on a little weight last summer and she says everybody is watching her waist to see if it stabilizes or keeps rising."

"Surely heaven will protect the working girl," I said.

"Yes. Heaven and you. I arranged for you to take Lucilla to town tomorrow for the nuts."

"A muchness of thanks, as we Mexicans say."

Next morning I presented myself at the store, where Lucilla presided at the cash register. She is not a languorous Latin *bella donna* with smoky eyes and a yard of black hair. She would, by gringo standards, be called a handsome woman. Her shoulders are square, her carriage erect, her face expressive. She has strong teeth, with gold in them.

The friends with whom she went to school are married now and almost all are overweight. Mexican wives get fatter, Mexican husbands get skinnier. Lucilla could well wear slacks, but does not. So far, only teen-agers or very young women dare appear in slacks here. Women wear dresses and when they get widowed, which so often does not take much time, they wear black dresses.

Lucilla will now almost certainly never marry. She is past thirty, she might even be approaching forty. Who could imagine a Mexican man, no matter what his age, marrying so old a woman? It would be unnatural, a flying in the face of nature.

"Good morning, Lucilla. We go now to Esquinapa."

She looked me straight and spoke me clearly. "*Where,*" she said, "is your *wife?*"

Enough is enough. "Dead," I said. I made my fingers into a pistol and blew my brains away with my thumb. "I shot her, so that you and I would not be disturbed."

She snorted. There hasn't been a murder here in years. But she didn't leave the cash register.

"Lucilla," I said, "I am going to town. If you want to get your pistachios, come to town. If not, stay here. But I am going to the town."

She eyed me in that direct, forceful manner that business-women have. "A moment," she said, and left the store in my care. Nobody seemed to want to buy from me, so we all waited for her return.

She came back accompanied by her sister-in-law, Eduviges. Eduviges is short, round, and funny. She is convinced that all creation is an unimaginably large, divine joke and that God truly loves only those who have a sense of humour.

"I am coming to help Lucilla carry the nuts, all six kilos of them," she said. She giggled and tumbled herself into the back seat. We drove away from the store.

"How did it go?" my wife asked when I returned two hours later.

"Eduviges had a thoroughly good time. She waved at her friends and traded jokes with people on the street. But Lucilla bent over as if she was picking up something from the floor and stayed that way until we were out of the village."

"Lucky for you Lucilla doesn't have a husband with a pistol," said my wife.

In a Mexican Line-up, Everybody Comes First

|||

TEACAPAN—Few national habits here so bewilder English-speaking people as the Mexicans' resolute, yea, even heroic resistance to lining up.

There are no queues here, except occasionally in some place where it doesn't matter.

When boarding a bus, Mexicans pack the doorway so tightly that it looks like a 1936 movie about the evacuation of Shanghai. Occasionally Mexicans will line up before a bank teller's wicket but most of the time the tellers face customers as a herd, and every one of those customers expects to be served ahead of whoever is being served.

At stores, at baseball games, and at Mass in the cathedral, the practice is the same. They are all like ants on a picnic cookie.

There is not much pushing or shoving. The Mexican sense of courtesy prevails. So does their sense of humour. People in these swarms chat, make jokes, and exchange gossip. They shout, amiably, at whatever salesperson they are trying to approach, even though that individual is either too harried to hear or too weary to respond.

What the crowd cannot, will not, and will never accept is the notion that the first should be first and the last last.

Nothing in the Canadian experience is so disorderly, with the sole exception of the Ottawa press gallery interviewing the nation's prime minister in a corridor outside the House of Commons. But those are press people, a notoriously undisciplined lot.

The average Canadian will cheerfully stand in line even to pay taxes, and believes that people who do not queue are indecent and maybe wicked besides.

I have just popped out of a pack of customers who descended upon Teller #1 at the Bancomer Bank in Esquinapa, being squeezed from that press like a seed from a lime. I had spent fifty-five minutes being brushed to one side by customers more agile or by customers who waved pieces of paper in their hands.

I was grateful when the teller, who had resolutely refused to make eye contact for fifty-five minutes, finally selected me while I was yet separated from her counter by the depth of two human bodies. If she had not chosen to catch my eye for another six minutes, the official time for exchanging money would have elapsed and I would have been turned away with no pesos.

In the banks it's not when you go to the teller that counts, it's when the teller selects you to be served. If you are not her choice, well, God makes other days, other tellers, and other banks. You must know that, don't you? You are over the age of twelve, aren't you?

When I was younger and understood everything there was to know about this nation, I calculated that Mexicans could not queue because of their pride. Pride is more important than money here.

The inability to form a queue could be explained by the fact that no Mexican is prepared to come second. Everybody comes first.

It is physically impossible for everybody to be served first. You know that. I know that. All the Mexicans know that. But it is just another of life's paradoxes, and we all learn to live with paradox.

To picture the Mexican system, think of the longest line-up you have ever seen. Then imagine that everybody is first in line.

These people stand before the tellers and the clerks as they stand before God, who says that all men are equal. What is good enough for God is good enough for the Mexican.

Having had time, a lot of time, one *hell* of a lot of time, for further observation of this phenomenon, I think there is a deeper social significance in the Mexican system than the Almighty may have noticed.

There is no better place to make the observations than at a

tortilla factory, which runs on bicycle chains, propane gas, and subsidized cornmeal. We have three in our village and from 10:00 A.M. until noon the stacks of little thin pancakes which are the staple food of this entire nation, and which taste like blotting paper, come flopping off the end of the production line to be dispensed to a nonqueueing crowd.

The crowd forms a familiar pattern. If you take the length of the sales counter for a diameter, the crowd will fill a semicircle of that diameter.

There is, as noted, little pushing or shoving and hardly ever any bad temper. Instead it's an occasion for much gossip among the women and occasionally some raunchy remarks. When a middle-aged man of senatorial girth pedals past on his bike, one of the women shouts, "Riding that bicycle around all the time, your testicles must be as flat as these tortillas." He waves in cheerful acknowledgement and pedals on, flattening them some more.

It is here, at the tortilla factory, that some order may be discerned among the disorder. More than order, there may even be purpose.

By not lining up, Mexicans tacitly acknowledge the reverse of what they seem to be proclaiming. All people are not born equal, no matter what any constitutional document may claim. Some are fast and some slow, some weak and some strong. Thus any salesperson in Mexico can redress some of the natural imbalance of society by serving the weak before the strong.

The same person may serve a friend before a stranger. That is also admirable, an example of the imperishable value of friendship.

At the tortilla factory nearest our house, no old lady will wait long to be served. Joanna, a big blonde woman whose ancestors came from Germany, will see that old lady and although she came last, she will be first. Joanna will prove what the Christian Bible claims, that the race is not always to the swift, neither the battle to the strong.

For different reasons, a woman with a crying baby who is disturbing people who want to gossip will also be served speedily and sent home with her brat. I wish some Mexican mother would lend me her baby so I could pack it around when I go shopping and pinch its bum when service is slow.

In the tortilla crowd there will be others, not visibly old, pregnant, or otherwise in need, who will make some kind of signal to Joanna, a signal that says that an emergency exists and this person truly needs speedy service. He or she will get it.

The system at the tortilla factory is hard on the kids, but instructive. A child at the tortilla factory will scarcely ever be served while there remains one adult who is waiting. Some children, sent to collect a family's morning tortilla stack, may wait half an hour and more while adults preempt their claim to service.

It's unfair to the kids. But remember, pray, that Mexicans adore children to distraction. If these people say that children must learn respect for elders, it is possible that some of us in other nations should listen.

It's a strange system, inefficient and by times unfair. But it is a system and not a random occurrence.

And even those of us who prefer, nay, long for a good old-fashioned and very British queue must remind ourselves that lining up has never established the New Jerusalem on our earth. Men lined up to die in trenches in the First World War and in gas chambers in the Second World War. Were we better for our orderly habits? Were we happier? Did we live longer?

Gas Station Kids

|||

TEACAPAN—A gas station in Mexico is usually a shabby place. The man who runs it obtained a licence from PEMEX, the state oil monopoly, which provides him reasonable protection against competition from other gas stations. You pretty well have to deal with him. He knows that.

Often there is no air for your tires and the pumps have not yet been recalibrated for the price increase of three months ago. You get used to that.

What is harder to get used to is a wild pack of little boys at these stations, each of whom demands the job of smearing a dirty rag across your windshield or pumping your gas for you.

They are weedy kids, ten to fourteen, and some are crippled or have scabies. They are as pushy, loud and insensitive to rebuff as the worst type of used car salesman in Canada.

They pay no attention to Mexican cars and Mexican car drivers ignore them utterly. The fellow citizens are at peace with one another.

However, the gas station gang can smell a gringo car two long hills distant and tell to the nearest five pesos how much money you have in your change purse. They race at your car while it is coasting into the pumps, hammering on the windows and sometimes flinging one of those filthy rags at your windshield to establish a claim for a wash job.

These rags are seldom if ever washed and reek of oil and tar.

Driving Mexican highways has its regular perils; the last thing you need is a smeared windshield.

"No, thank you," you say. "Thanks, but no thank you." "No, THANK you." "NO, thank you." "NO, THANK YOU!"

Politeness can work with a professional beggar in a tourist centre such as Mazatlán. "GOOD morning," you say, brightly, in English. "GOOD morning. GOOD morning." You have been obtuse in failing to see the outstretched hand, but pleasantly obtuse. After a couple of repetitions the professional beggar knows there is no money to be had from you and will leave you.

Not PEMEX station kids. They have no use for courtliness. They want money. They want ball-point pens. Five gringos may reject them but they know there is a sixth who will poke money out the window to be rid of them and since he may not yet know the value of Mexican money the profit can be handsome.

So they persist and finally the gringo addresses them in short, pungent Anglo-Saxon words. The kids then withdraw and form a ring around the car with small, dark faces hardset. You would not want them touching the valve stems on the tires.

After a while you learn to avoid PEMEX stations where the children are thickest and drive farther to find smaller stations where the kids are fewer, frailer or more easily discouraged.

You become hardened. A callus forms over the heart. The more fat around your heart, the quicker the callus forms.

In Mexico, you are rich and you easily learn the ways of those who are rich at home in Canada. You pride yourself on not giving alms because, as Abraham Lincoln explained, you cannot help a man by giving him things. Mr. Lincoln said no such thing, but a rich man's hireling wrote the forgery a generation ago and by constant repetition it has attained a form of authenticity. Ordinary people, particularly Moslems and Christians, feel uneasy when they deny charity but the rich are righteous in their selfishness, they know they are improving the characters of poor people and making the nation stronger.

Bah. Humbug. Are there no jails? Are there no poorhouses?

Then you are reminded of what you would rather not remember. Some truths become inescapable in Mexico.

The kids seldom if ever are begging. They are all insisting on selling you a service. It may be poor service. It may be spurious service. But it is a service. And although the boys are noisy, aggressive and rude they have not surrendered to poverty. They have not sunk into apathy. They do not whine.

Now and then a gringo on a Mexican street may encounter a child who follows him saying, "Do you have a present for me? I am poor. I am very poor. Do you have a present for me?" The same child may be wheeling a bicycle, something half the kids don't have, but in the begging trade that doesn't seem to matter. He has learned the beggar's trick of abject self-pity and that terrible persistence. He is not like a gas station boy.

There are little girls among the gas station kids. They do not try to wash windshields, although they would probably do the job as it should be done. Some sexual ordering of jobs forbids them that.

Usually they are carrying trays of flyblown candy, sticks of sugar cane hard as bamboo or something else unappetizing and unwholesome.

They do not have the aggressiveness of the boys. They stand in silent melancholy beside your window until, their silence met by yours, they leave in eloquent silent despair.

I sent such a one away at Christmastime once and when she went over and stood forlorn beside the dirty stucco wall I reflected that neither I nor any of my children had ever been asked to sell slop to arrogant foreigners. Also, she was a girl. You can snarl at boys but girls are different.

So I walked over and put some money in her hand. No, thank you, I said, I didn't want to buy, this was a Christmas present.

The amount I don't remember and it would mean little today anyway because in times of currency inflation peso values mean little across the months and years. It was, perhaps, ten times what she was asking for her sweetstuff but she was asking almost nothing and ten times almost nothing is almost nothing.

"What did you give her?" asked the American who was riding in my car that morning. I told him.

"I hope she has enough sense to hide it from her mother," he said.

Mexican Low Finance

|||

TEACAPAN—The bankers, the politicians, all the important and useful people, keep talking about Mexican High Finance, and how it brought the world's big banks close to collapse.

Nobody in our village understands high finance. Maybe that is proof that nobody here is important or useful or capable of collapsing the world's economic system. I wouldn't know. Even in the Mexican republic I retain my title, Non-Economist.

What I know is that in our village, we use Mexican Low Finance. Mexican Low Finance is much more complicated than you might think. In fact, there are gringos in our area who have been studying Low Finance for decades, and they still haven't quite spotted the trick of it.

When you deal with Low Finance in Mexico you are faced squarely with a contradiction of the Mexican character, and there is no escape from that contradiction.

On the one hand, money is important because it keeps you from dying. Villages such as the one we live in are poor to a degree that few Canadians ever knew or could remember if they did know. Statistically, it could be proven that most of our town cannot buy enough food for their families on the money they earn.

However, set against this terrible need to get enough money to live, there is the traditional Mexican view that money is vulgar stuff. Money is something like hemorrhoids. Maybe you have some, lots of people do, but, please, there are other subjects for conversation.

The response to this contradiction in the national character is Low Finance.

If you would study Low Finance, consider Victor, Victor's wife, Victor's bicycle, the Communist Party of Mexico, a village named Christ the King, the Mexican police, and the Mexican press. They all are part of the system.

Victor is an electrician. In a dawn-to-dark working day, he earns about one-half of what a Canadian electrician earns in one hour. Victor, his wife, and two small children live in a house that doesn't amount to much more than two rooms and one bougainvillea vine. He rides a bicycle. Frequently you may see Victor pedalling the bicycle down the main street while balancing his ladder on his shoulder. It is not easy. Try it sometime.

Victor undertook to be our contractor when we built a small addition to our house.

"Before we start, Victor," I said, "let's settle how you will be paid. Do you want to be paid by the hour? Do you want a fee for the job? Do you want a percentage of money spent on the job?"

Money, said Victor, we could discuss later. Money was not a matter of importance, he said.

Mexicans are charming people, but they can be exasperating. They will provide you street directions even if they have not the remotest notion of where the streets run, because if you are asked for directions it is polite to give some. Ask them if your car can be fixed and they will always say yes, because yes is what you wish to hear. Ask one about payment of money and, unless he is a banker or a beach boy, his eyes will become opaque and he will change the subject.

There are times when the gringo says to hell with these charming ways.

"To hell with that, Victor," I said, in the best Spanish I can manage. "Money is important. It is truly, truly important material. And what are you anyway, some kind of a Communist?"

At this he laughed, which is unusual. He tends to be a sardonic individual.

"I dislike the Communists just as much as I dislike all other politicians," he said, "but it's a funny thing that you should say this."

The previous year, it turned out, Victor served as a bill collector for Mexican hydro. In the neighbouring village named Christ the King, where more than the usual number of house walls bear the legend "This Household Votes Communist," Victor had advised hydro's customers to refuse to pay their bills because their service was so poor.

One thing led to another. The police were called. They threw Victor in their paddy wagon.

The villagers of Christ the King turned out and removed Victor from the wagon.

This news was later to be carried in the nearest weekly newspaper and also broadcast on the radio, two events that may say more than anything else about the changing political climate of Mexico. However, in our little area news travels fastest by word of mouth. By the time Victor got home that night, his wife knew about the riot in Christ the King.

"She kept saying, 'You are a Communist. Everybody says that you are a Communist.' She was extremely turbulent."

"What did you say, Victor?" I asked.

He gave me one of those looks by which Mexicans measure the immense difference between themselves and gringos.

"I said, 'Be silent, woman, and bring me my dinner.' "

By this time all hopes of financial negotiation, high or low, were lost for the day.

Victor took over as our contractor. For two months he used a significant part of his working week to hire and fire labour, find materials, buy materials, cajole truckers to make deliveries, and supervise workmanship.

The day before our departure for Canada I said: "Victor, the time has arrived when you and I must discuss money, whether you like to or not."

Our bougainvillea, he observed, would not flower well unless we tied it over the top of the patio wall.

"Money, Victor," I said. "Pesos. Dollars. Money."

"Whatever it is worth to you," said Victor.

Nothing is more difficult than the Mexican dealing in Low Finance. "How can I repay you for saving my life?" says the gringo. "Whatever it is worth to you," answers the Mexican.

As Victor and I both knew, I had here the opportunity to cheat him shamefully. I would never get the chance to cheat him or anybody else in the village again, but I had this opportunity.

I might, on the other hand, overpay him by an extravagant amount. That is a much less serious offence against morals and manners but it can, in extremes, be offensive. Heavy overpayment indicates that Mexican money and Mexicans mean nothing to you. It is not a good reputation to have in a community where there are so many Mexicans and so few gringos.

While my wife and Victor discussed flowers, I calculated the total wages and material costs of the job, estimated Victor's pay at a common Canadian formula, 10 per cent of the job, added some more pesos, by guess, put it all in an unsealed envelope, and passed it over to him. It was an amount significant in his annual income.

"Thanks," he said. More commonly the Mexican says "Many thanks" but Victor is, as I say, laconic.

He poked the envelope in his shirt pocket and, half an hour later, left our house with the envelope unopened, the amount of payment unknown to him and uncounted. He trusted we should meet again, one year hence. He pedalled away on the rusty old bicycle, which is going to fall apart underneath him one of these days.

Corvina in the Surf

|||

TEACAPAN—As I kick off my sandals at the edge of the beach this morning an angel comes up and says, "Rejoice and be glad, sir, for this is a day the Lord hath made for you." I knew it was going to be that kind of day when I submerged the first cup of coffee.

I thank the angel for letting me know and ask, politely, that a reminder be dropped that the Koran states that Allah does not deduct from a man's allotted life span the hours that he spends in fishing. Reminders, the angel says, are not necessary: Heaven's gatekeeper is himself a fisherman of note from the Sea of Galilee.

It all helps, this sort of thing. To catch fish without faith is extremely difficult, and omens and visitations are what build faith.

The other good omens attached to this day in January include a moon which is just right, being new and strong, and a tide which is also just right, being higher than usual and coinciding with the dawn.

And when I turned an ear seaward this morning, the sound of the sea was a Fisherman's Sound. The Fisherman's Sound is like the Hunter's Moon, confusing to those who don't hunt or fish. A Hunter's Moon is no moon; the game animals can't feed during the dark nights and so come out by day when they may be found. The Fisherman's Sound is no sound. If, from our house, I cannot hear the surf pound on the nearest beach, The Drum, it means that the ocean swells are low, slow and syrupy and that I shall be able to cast out into clear blue water.

On this morning, nothing could be heard from The Drum. There were only the usual yawn and stretch sounds of a Mexican village waking to a new day. Farm tractors muttered. Yamaha outboards hummed in the lagoon where the shark fishermen were leaving for a day on the ocean. From the plaza the tinny little bell of our tinny little church went ding, ding to summon some of the old Mexican ladies in black to morning Mass. And, of course, there were the sounds of dogs fighting, roosters crowing and the jack burro singing about love.

It was black and cold when I wheeled the car out through our big, iron carport gate and poked along through the patches of ground fog in the coconut and mango groves. I passed by The Drum and continued on to a section of beach ten kilometres farther north which we gringos call The Wreck. At The Wreck there is the hulk of a steel shrimp boat. It is completely covered by water at this tide. In the predawn darkness, I shall have to try to cast right or left of it by hope and instinct. Some days the wreck takes more of my lures than the corvina do.

Wreck Beach's sands are still cold enough to make the bare feet ache. It is hard to remember that here at the southern end of the state of Sinaloa we are in the tropics, the village of Teacapan lying about 150 kilometres south of the invisible line of Cancer. When I checked the outdoor thermometer in our yard it read a chill twelve degrees. Seattle or Vancouver mightn't be any colder at this hour of a winter day. But then comes the experience which never fails to surprise those of us who come from the shores of the Pacific Northwest—I walk into the water to warm my feet. The water, for more than two weeks now, has been a most comforting twenty-two degrees.

Even in the uncertain pearly light before the dawn, I can see that the swells are coming in to the shore wrapped in satin, whispering of the deeps. They thump occasionally and there is a confusion of spray, foam, and sand, but on this day, almost any old rod could throw an ounce of Kastmaster lure into clear water. I'm carrying a longer, stiffer rod than most, glass and exotic fibres whose names I can't remember, eleven feet long, made for me by Wayne Hansen of New Westminster. He and I used up some of the previous summer and fall arguing about this rod. He puts comparatively narrow guides on casting rods; I claim that the line out of a big open-faced reel should peel through at least the first and second guides with scarcely a kiss for the metal. Oh well, Hansen is as Hansen does and I end up with a rod fitted with small guides. Admittedly, it has turned out to cast farther and easier than any other surf rod I have used, so possibly he knew what he was doing.

There is a dusky blush in the eastern sky when I throw the Kastmaster at the sea but it goes farther than I can see. I can only sense by the slack in the 6.5 kilo line that it has hit and is winking down into dark waters.

I give the lure time to sink and then retrieve it. How fast? How slow? No one has ever been certain. You reel, lift the rod tip to change the lure's speed and action, drop the rod, reel again. If it comes in too slowly it will appear dead and corvina will scorn it. If it comes in too fast it won't seem worth the fish's while to chase it because all fish, orangemouth corvina included, must calculate their feeding practices to ensure that they spend fewer calories to catch feed than the food can supply to them.

So, at the right moment or the wrong, you strike the fish. If you are too early you will snatch it from him and if too late he will already have mouthed the lure and spit it out. Should you be skillful or lucky, you will strike at just the right moment and the rod tip will turn down to the ocean's face like a willow switch in the hands of a douser witching for well water.

You may still lose him. Quite likely you will. Often as not the corvina will snap at a lure in irritation rather than in hunger and the hook just nicks one corner of the mouth, from which it is easily dislodged in the ensuing water sports.

On my third retrieve this morning, somebody who I never see taps the side of my rod with a silver dollar. Next the rod tip jigs and quivers. The corvina prefers to fool around with a lure before striking. The sharp tap which precedes the quiver puzzled me for many seasons but in time I discovered the answer—my Daiwa reel is worn in the gears and when a fish first interferes with the retrieve there is a snap as the gears are braked.

I lose three fish while there are still stars in the sky. Then the sun, in tropic style, flings itself up from the crests of the Sierra Madre mountains, for all the world as if it had slept through the alarm. Full daylight, blue sky and cruising squadrons of pelicans are created out of the darkness within minutes.

The fourth fish does not knock to announce himself but charges the lure and comes completely out of the water with it, throwing diamonds all around him in the new sunlight. That's the way they are. Sometimes hesitant as a June bride, other times more like a freight train. This corvina runs, jumps again, then runs towards the beach. All I can do is crank frantically and hope there will still be weight on the line after the slack is taken up. He runs down the beach and I run with him.

Finally he peels line on a long run to seaward and a strange thing occurs. Far out beyond the wreck another corvina breaks water. Then I see where the rod is bending and, by damn, that's MY fish out there surfacing. He has pulled a couple of hundred metres off the reel and soon he'll continue on his way to New Zealand.

All I can do is bear down on the drag and reflect that if he breaks the line he deserves to go and reproduce fish that are big and strong like himself. But he doesn't break the line. He starts coming in and makes only a few more short rushes. He is tiring. Finally, I can see him in the wave just beyond the breaking wave and it is clear that he is beginning to cast himself on his beam ends.

So he comes to the final wave, the wave where most corvina are lost. I want this to be a big wave. What's the saying, every seventh wave is a big one? Maybe it's true.

I run out into the thrash of the water, get him right under the rod tip, screw the drag to the last notch and then, as that final wave breaks and runs up the sloping beach I run with it and the corvina comes with me. I hold him as the water retreats, leaving him flapping on the wet sand. Half of them will throw the hook at this point, but unless another and larger wave comes hurrying in there is time to grab the fish at the back of the gills and drag him out of the ocean's reach.

Like the North Pacific salmon, the corvina has a blue-green sheen to his scales when fresh from the water, although this colour soon fades. In many ways he resembles the salmon, particularly the spring salmon which is the largest species of the Pacific. Like the spring, he usually takes hesitantly, tugging and towing instead of racing around, and he usually makes swirls at the surface rather than jumping clear of the water as a coho salmon will. His body is salmon-shaped although the tail terminates in a diamond shape instead of being square. His flesh is white, not pink.

This fish is almost four kilos in weight and 750 millimetres long. Not small but also not big. I have landed corvina here of eight kilos who measured a full metre. The largest known to be caught locally on rod and line was one and a half metres in length and weighed probably fifteen kilos.

There are other fish to be caught here, too. The California corvina, which rarely exceeds two kilos in weight, is another of the eight varieties which occur locally. There is also a fish shaped like a full moon, called toro because the placement of its head is such that it resembles the classic fighting bull with its horns down for a charge. Toros never leap but, kilo for kilo, they are harder to land than corvina because they can turn broadside to the waves and wear down an angler who tries to shift them from that position.

Even harder to beach are the manta rays. If their wings span a metre, you might as well cut the line and say goodbye Charlie because no surf rod will drag them to the shore.

There are pargo, big rose-coloured fish which some gringos call red snapper but which to others seem more to resemble monster bass. There are ocean catfish, which live cheerfully in these broiling waters and use three sharp spines to poison the unwary or the unlucky. There are robalo, called snook in American waters. Pound for pound, the robalo outfights all others. On a day when you bring a robalo to the beach you are entitled to be simply rotten in your behaviour to other fishermen.

There are fish not for the catching, such as the dancing sharks which come out of the water like ballerinas. Usually they are far at sea but sometimes they come near the shores and you do not wade to your waist then when you fish. And there are the porpoises. Sometimes, wading far from shore at low tide, you can coax a porpoise to come in beside you by brushing the water with your hand. They know it's a trick, but porpoises like having fun. Think of the friendliest, the jolliest uncle you had when you were a kid. That's a porpoise.

But corvina is the staple surf fish for the rod-and-reel man. We have enough theories and superstitions about corvina fishing to supply a whole religion.

One gringo who sometimes fishes near me showed me statistics he had kept on corvina fishing, and these showed that 95 per cent of all the corvina he ever caught he brought to shore before 8:00 A.M.; also that 78 per cent of these were caught with a silver Crocodile lure and 22 per cent with a green Crocodile. I was only fifty-nine when he told me that and not as wise as I am now. I have since discovered that he has scarcely ever fished past 8:00 A.M. on any day and that the only lures he owns are Crocodiles. They were perfect statistics, impeccably accurate and utterly useless.

Some people catch more fish than other people. An American who from time to time fishes next to me on the beach invariably strikes more fish than I do and lands more. We use the same lure, and as far as anyone can perceive, the same techniques in the same waters.

From time to time there is a Mexican sport fisherman who outdoes both of us. We made a point of looking at the lure he used. I can testify that it caught fish like hell but apart from that it didn't amount to much.

There are many days, more than I care to think about, when nobody catches anything in the surf. There are ten adjectives which describe days like those but nine are grossly indecent and the tenth is too insipid to be worth uttering.

There are days too good for the fun of anybody except a commercial fisherman, days when porpoises or other predators bloody the water among the bait-fish and the corvina go into a feeding frenzy. At such times they will eat anything that moves and sometimes come right up on the beach and chase the fishermen back among the coconut palms trying to snatch lures out of their pockets.

On this day, the fishing is perfect, which includes being not too good. I take four corvina, all of more than three kilos, and lose five others in the friendly sea.

As I leave the beach that morning, shortly before 7:30, the porpoises come in, bodysurfing on the swells near the beach and sometimes hurling themselves out of the water and seeing who can make the biggest dent in the Pacific Ocean. Nobody knows for sure why porpoises do this but I know that porpoises, like human fishermen, sometimes have fun for reasons which are obscure.

The Republic v. Dan McGrew

|||

TEACAPAN—Down here in the Spanish-Indian realm, where men's ways seem often strange, I am reminded of Bob Bouchette, who had some strange ways himself.

Bob Bouchette was one of the greatest of many columnists on the *Vancouver Sun*. His was an early trumpet call in a grand flourish of vivid writing in Vancouver newspapers. The city was to become noted not for the excellence of its press, which must ever be a subjective judgement and endlessly debatable, but for the strong personalities of the newspapers and the people who served on them.

Vancouver was the town where you might pick up a newspaper and discover that the collapse of a Canadian government the previous day had not been noted on the editorial pages. However, your heart might lift to read in the *Province* James Butterfield's column on spring that began: "Er—spring / You perfectly priceless old thing . . ."

I never knew Bob Bouchette. He died, a suicide, during the Second World War, a few years before I first saw Vancouver. He had left a multitude of debts and about as many friends, a reputation as a writer which we all envied, and some great unwritten stories.

At one time, faced with imminent bankruptcy, Bob invited all his creditors to an expensive dinner, where he explained to them that not only could he not pay them a cent, he couldn't pay for the dinner either, and would they please be good enough to pick up the bill.

One of the stories that attached to him was of a great confrontation between Bob and the Mexican republic. It may be mere legend. I cannot say. I know it is believable.

It was during the early thirties. Bob was temporarily not in the writing business on account of having forgotten to do it, gotten drunk, or been fired, all of which were things that happened to him from time to time. He and a friend hitchhiked into Mexico. They got drunk and became hostile to policemen in some little Mexican village in Chihuahua or Durango, and were taken to keep the fleas company in the local dungeon.

After a day or two they were brought to court, unshaven, unfresh, unshriven, and generally unlovely of appearance. There they heard the evidence against them, all of which was in Spanish.

They knew a few dozen words of Spanish, but didn't admit to it. Any man who tries to use an unfamiliar language in a court proceeding deserves what he gets, which may be hanging. Bob had seen many French-Canadians, moderately fluent in English, who became totally ignorant of the language when in a courtroom. He knew survival techniques.

The two Canadian prisoners sat mute, and Mexican law and Mexican lawyers rolled over them.

"Leave it to me," said Bob, speaking between his teeth.

There came a time in the proceedings when the Mexican republic appeared to have exhausted all of its antagonism towards the Canadians. Without words, there being none mutually comprehensible, it was indicated to Bob that he might offer a defence, poor thing though it might be.

He stood, not weak, bewildered and alone, no, nor at that moment noticeable for his dirty clothes, his lack of acquaintance with a razor, and his powerful underarm odours. He stood straight and waited, as any good actor must, for the silence and attention he required. When that dusty little courtroom became still, when every eye was turned to him, Bob began his statement for the defence: " 'A bunch of the boys were whooping it up in the Malamute saloon; / The kid that handles the music box was hitting a jag-time tune . . .' "

He recited every word of *The Shooting of Dan McGrew*. It was one of the talents he had held for years, unknown to his fellow newspapermen in Vancouver. This was the only time it ever proved useful.

Think on it. It does not matter whether you like Robert Service. Think of the gestures, the pitch of voice, the light of eye, the toss of hair and head which are appropriate to that old Yukon ballad. Imagine what these would seem to mean if you did not know a word that was being spoken: " '. . . But I want to state, and my words are straight, and I'll bet my poke they're true, / That one of you is a hound of hell . . . and that one is Dan McGrew.' "

The Mexicans not only freed them. They wept for them, they applauded them, and the magistrate gave Bob the double embrace with kisses on both cheeks.

So goes the story of Bouchette in Mexico, and I can believe it all. I could believe it equally were it true that the magistrate, privily, was entirely fluent in the English language and had the collected works of Robert Service in his home.